Balance Sheet Basics for Nonfinancial Managers

Balance Sheet Basics for Nonfinancial Managers

Joseph Peter Simini

Certified Public Accountant
Emeritus Professor of Accounting

WILEY

JOHN WILEY & SONS
NEW YORK · CHICHESTER · BRISBANE
TORONTO · SINGAPORE

This book is dedicated to Dr. Mithileshwar Singh and to the memory of B. J. Anderson; Richard L. Hanlin, C.P.A.; John C. Messershmidt, C.P.A.; Dr. Oswald Neilsen; and Dr. John Pagani.

ISBN 0-471-61418-1; ISBN 0-471-61833-0 (pbk.)

Printed in the United States of America

10 9 8 7 6 5 4 3 2 1

Preface

In my experience, many people in business find financial statements intimidating. Often these people are managers or even owners of businesses. They have access to large amounts of organized financial information, yet they are unsure how to use the information creatively to increase profitability.

A financial statement—such as a balance sheet, an income statement, or a statement of changes in financial position—is a concise, condensed summary of accounting data. Accounting is often called the language of business. It records transactions that affect financial records. (There are some transactions that accounting does not record; for example, it does not record the signing of a contract for a wholesaler to carry a manufacturer's line of merchandise.) In the traditional sense, accounting tells only what has happened that can be shown in money terms. It is possible, however, to look at financial statements and discern underlying problems or opportunities. A regular review of financial records can disclose qualitative dimensions of a company's operating practices. This kind of review may enable a manager to solve problems or to introduce new, profit-enhancing procedures.

My goal in this book is to help you become a creative reader of one of the key financial statements: the balance sheet. The book begins with an introduction to the balance sheet as a whole. Chapters then cover current and long-lived (fixed) assets, current and long-term liabilities, and owners' equity. The final chapter presents a selection of ratios often used to analyze and interpret financial statements. In each chapter I focus on operational issues, suggesting ways to improve control, avert problems, and increase efficiency.

Each chapter offers one or more "examples" embodying concepts discussed in the chapter. The situations described in the examples are extremely simplified—they are intended to convey general ideas, not to teach bookkeeping or accounting procedures. You are encouraged to keep pencil, paper, and calculator at hand and test your acumen through the examples as you go along.

No book is written from idea to completed manuscript without changes and revisions. This volume is no different. My love to my wife, Marcelline, who listens to my dreams and gives me the room to make them come true.

Other have also helped in the writing of this book. There are those in my university who assigned me to teach Accounting 1A and 1B, principles of accounting, and other accounting theory courses. There are my students, who helped me restructure the materials with their questions. Not least there are the creators of the computer programs that make writing so much easier. To all of these I owe my thanks. Writing this book was an enjoyable experience. I hope that reading it will be equally enjoyable, and helpful.

San Francisco, California   JOSEPH PETER SIMINI
January, 1990

Contents

Part I: Introduction

Chapter 1: The Balance Sheet 3
What is a balance sheet? 4
The income statement 6
Footnotes and other information 10
Why should we study balance sheets? 12
Examples 13
Summary 16

Part II: Assets

Chapter 2: Cash 21
What is cash? 22
What is cash flow? 23
Protection of cash assets 24
Examples 33
Summary 37

Chapter 3: Receivables 41
What are receivables? 41
Types of credit 42
Granting credit 44

Problems with issuing credit   45
Recognizing losses from receivables   50
Using outside credit   53
Examples   54
Summary   57

Chapter 4: Inventories   59
What are inventories?   60
Types of inventory   61
Valuation of inventories   63
Control of inventories   68
Examples   76
Summary   79

Chapter 5: Long-lived Assets   81
What are long-lived assets?   82
Types and values of long-lived assets   82
Methods of depreciation   86
Leasing versus buying   95
Disposal of long-lived assets   96
Example   99
Summary   101

Part III: Liabilities

Chapter 6: Current Payables   105
What are current payables?   106
Control matters   106
Discounts and timing of payments   110
Example   112
Summary   113

Chapter 7: Long-term Debt   115
What is long-term debt?   115
Types of long-term debt   117
Special considerations with long-term debt   122
Other long-term liabilities   123
Example   125
Summary   129

Part IV: Equity
  Chapter 8: Owners' Equity 133
    What is owners' equity? 134
    Forms of equity in different organizations 134
    Examples 145
    Summary 149

Part V: Analyzing Financial Statements
  Chapter 9: Analyzing Financial Ratios 153
    What are financial ratios? 154
    Liquidity and turnover ratios 156
    Leverage ratios 160
    Profitability ratios 162
    Example 165
    Summary 169
  Glossary 171
  Index 177

PART

I

Introduction

1 The Balance Sheet

You may already know more about balance sheets than you are aware. Have you ever made a list of the dollar value of the things you own and set this list against a list of your debts? If all is well, you have enough money to pay your debts, plus something in reserve, without having to sell your car or other possessions.

Companies make the same kinds of lists at regular intervals. But in the business world, these lists are called balance sheets. A company balance sheet may be brief and simple, or it may be fairly elaborate and amply footnoted. The basic components of all balance sheets are the same, however. As you become familiar with these components, you will find that you are able to understand and make use of balance sheet information.

A company regularly compiles not only a balance sheet but an income statement. The income statement is the subject of *Profit and Loss Basics for Nonfinancial Managers*, planned as a sequel to this book. But the income statement makes several appearances here, because we use the balance sheet, the income statement, and other information together to evaluate the health of a business. Thus, a brief introduction to the income statement and other relevant items appears later in this chapter.

WHAT IS A BALANCE SHEET?

A balance sheet is a record of the assets, liabilities, and equity of a business as of a particular date. A balance sheet does not aim to depict ongoing company activities; it is not a movie but a freeze-frame. Its purpose is to depict the dollar value of various components of the business at a moment in time. For example, a turkey farm's inventory (turkey supply) will shrink drastically at Thanksgiving. Therefore, the "inventory" items on the farm's balance sheets in October and December will be very different.

The term *balance sheet* has a long history and is in widespread use. There are several alternative names for the same document, among them *statement of financial condition* and *statement of financial position*. But since the term balance sheet is both concise and customary, I'll use it in this book.

A balance sheet consists of two lists (see exhibit 1.1). By accounting tradition, the left-hand list shows the company's assets; the right-hand list includes the company's liabilities plus the owners' equity. The two sides of a balance sheet must always have equal dollar amounts—they must "balance."

Assets are valuable items owned by a business, whether fully paid for or not. These include cash and its equivalents; accounts receivable, or amounts due to be paid to the company; inventories; property, plant, and equipment; and other financial assets, such as deposits or prepayments held by other businesses. Chapters 2 through 5 discuss the different types of assets.

Liabilities are obligations to nonowners—individuals or organizations with no ownership interest in the company's trade transactions—for goods or services. These nonowners have advanced money, goods, or services to the company and must be reimbursed in cash at mutually agreed upon times. Typical liabilities include accounts payable, payroll, and short- and long-term debt to lenders and investors.

A balance sheet subdivides assets and liabilities into current and noncurrent categories. For example, *current assets* are cash and other assets that can be converted to cash or used within one year of the balance sheet date. *Current liabilities* (see chapter 6) are those that are due and payable within one year. These balance sheet entries can reveal, to an extent, information about a company's short-term strength. If current liabilities exceed current assets, the business may have difficulty meeting its payment obligations within the year. In fact, some experts feel that in a well-run company current assets should be approximately double current liabilities. Noncurrent ("long-lived") assets are those with a productive or economic life of more than one year, including property, plant, and equipment, as discussed in chapter 5. Noncurrent (long-term) liabilities are debts to lenders, mortgage holders, bondholders, and certain other creditors with maturities of more than one year (see chapter 7).

Equity, or net worth, is what a business owes to its owner(s). Equity is a residual figure, representing the book value of the business's assets once all liabilities have been satisfied. It is important to realize, however, that the balance sheet figure for equity may not accurately reflect the present-day market value of a company's assets. (Chapter 5 explains why.)

The reason balance sheets are structured as they are lies in the early history of *double-entry accounting* (accounting that balances every credit with a debit). As businesses became more complex—moving away from all-cash transactions, capitalizing long-lived assets, and charging off the cost of long-lived assets to operations over their useful lives—it became apparent that one category of owned property was not enough. Thus the breakdown into current and long-lived assets came about. The liabilities side of the sheet was also subdivided to show what the business owed to nonowners (liabilities) and what it owed to owners (equity).

As mentioned above, the two halves of a balance sheet must always add up to the same dollar amount. This balancing act reflects the basic equation of all accounting:

Assets = Liabilities + Equity

Keep in mind, though, that by definition equity is the value of assets once all liabilities have been satisfied. Creditors have a *superior claim* on assets: Creditors must receive what is owed them before the business's owners can claim anything.

You may have noticed that this listing of the items on a balance sheet omits some things that many people consider valuable "assets" in business. For example, many people consider a fine reputation, an experienced staff, and high employee loyalty and morale to be valuable assets. But these kinds of items do not appear on a balance sheet, because accounting conventions do not allow for their inclusion; they are *nonfinancial assets*. A balance sheet lists only *financial assets*.

Exhibits 1.1 and 1.2 show two types of balance sheets. The "account form" of balance sheet, exhibit 1.1, has the assets on the left and the liabilities and equity on the right, the conventional double-entry accounting arrangement. Exhibit 1.2 is the type of arrangement you will encounter in a typical annual report and is called the "report form" of balance sheet.

THE INCOME STATEMENT

Whereas a balance sheet reflects the condition of a company on a particular day, an *income statement* shows the results of

Exhibit 1.1   Account Form of Balance Sheet

Pierson Company
Balance Sheet
December 31, 19X6

ASSETS		LIABILITIES AND EQUITY	
Current assets:		Current liabilities:	
Cash	$ 10,000	Accounts payable	$ 50,000
Accounts receivable	20,000	Current long-term debt	75,000
Total current assets	30,000	Total current liabilities	125,000
Plant assets:		Noncurrent liabilities:	
Land	50,000		
Building	490,000		
Equipment	235,000	Long-term debt	236,000
	775,000	Total liabilities	361,000
Less: accumulated depreciation	294,000	Total equity*	182,000
Total plant assets	481,000		
Other assets	32,000	Total liabilities and equity	$543,000
Total assets	$543,000		

*Total equity varies in format according to type of ownership.

operations over the whole fiscal period (usually a year) between the beginning and ending balance sheet dates. Other terms for an income statement include profit-and-loss statement, earnings report, operations statement, and operating statement.

The income statement matches amounts received from goods or services and other items of income against all the

Exhibit 1.2   Report Form of Balance Sheet

Pierson Company
Balance Sheet
December 31, 19X6

ASSETS

Current assets:

Cash		$ 10,000	
Accounts receivable		20,000	
Total current assets			$ 30,000
Long-lived assets:			
Land		50,000	
Building	$490,000		
Less: accumulated depreciation	172,000	318,000	
Equipment	235,000		
Less: accumulated depreciation	122,000	113,000	
Total long-lived assets			481,000
Other assets			32,000
Total assets			$543,000

LIABILITIES AND EQUITY

Current liabilities:

Accounts payable	$ 50,000
Current portion of long-term debt	75,000
Total current liabilities	125,000
Long-term liabilities:	
Real estate mortgage (noncurrent portion)	236,000
Total liabilities	361,000
Total equity (varies in format according to type of ownership)	182,000
Total liabilities and equity	$543,000

costs and outlays incurred in order to operate the company and generate income during the period. The fiscal period's results may show a *profit*, or excess of income over related expenses. Or they may show a *loss*, an excess of related expenses over income. The income statement can be summarized as an equation:

Income for period − Related expenses for period = Profit (or loss) for period

Income statements vary according to the type of business. A service business has the simplest form of income statement. A merchandising business, such as a supermarket or department store, uses a more detailed statement, because it carries inventories of goods ready for sale. A manufacturer has the most complex income statement, because a manufacturer changes the shape and/or utility of materials to create new products for business or individual consumer use. Manufacturers' income statements, accordingly, have schedules showing expenditures of raw materials, labor, and overhead on goods in the process of production.

Exhibit 1.3, the income statement of Thomas Johnson Sales, a merchandising business, shows the income statement in a fairly simple, condensed form. Notice the basic categories of information, which appear on all income statements.

The income statement fits together with the balance sheet to form a coherent history of the business enterprise. For example, various assets shown on the balance sheet may change because of purchases or other expenses incurred during the period. A key link is the equity section of the balance sheet. Since changes in equity from the beginning to the ending balance sheet reflect profits or losses for the period, these equity changes connect the balance sheet with the bottom line of the income statement.

Exhibit 1.3   Income Statement

Thomas Johnson Sales
Statement of Income and Expense
For Year 19X3

Income from sales		$475,000
Cost of goods sold		227,000
Gross profit		248,000
Expenses:		
Sales salaries	$80,000	
Office salaries	32,000	
Payroll taxes	7,400	
Insurance	9,000	
Auto expense	27,000	
Depreciation	18,000	
Telephone	2,500	
Office supplies and postage	6,200	
Rent	16,000	
Other taxes	2,000	200,100
Net income		$ 47,900

FOOTNOTES AND OTHER INFORMATION

A company's formal balance sheet and income statement presentations are concise and condensed. Whenever a complex situation calls for explanation, that explanation appears in a footnote to the financial statement. So be sure to read footnotes; they often contain vital information that appears nowhere else. A few examples of the kinds of information that may be footnoted are:

- Accounting adjustments for inflation
- Inventory valuation method—first-in, first-out (FIFO) or last-in, first-out (LIFO) (see chapter 4)
- Changes in the company's method of depreciating long-lived assets (see chapter 5)

- Details of a company's plans to redeem a long-term liability
- Contingent liabilities, representing claims or lawsuits pending (see chapter 7)
- Long-term leases (see chapter 7)
- Details of employment benefits, profit sharing, and pension and retirement plans (see chapter 7)
- Changes in the value of issued stock (see chapter 8) because of stock dividends or splits
- Details of stock options granted to officers and employees
- Changes in percentage holdings, possibly reflecting an investor or group of investors positioning themselves for a takeover attempt

Many other kinds of information that are not required to be spelled out in financial statements can sometimes be deduced by the well-informed reader. For example, a company may have been forced by litigation to upgrade its facilities to meet occupational safety codes or to reduce toxic waste emissions. In the annual report, by way of explaining an increase in the dollar value of certain assets, the company may allude to an "equipment modernization program." The explanation may discuss the installation of the new equipment, the impact of the new equipment on the company's competitiveness, and so on. Occasionally, the letter from the chairman of the board or the president that accompanies the financial statements may clarify why the new equipment was necessary.

In many cases, however, it's up to the alert reader to fill in the details. A well-informed reader of financial statements also reads general newspapers, watches television news, reads the *Wall Street Journal* and business and industry periodicals. Indeed, information is such an important commodity in the business world that "information brokers" now offer their services to subscribers. They provide (for a fee) comprehensive databases, categorized and classified and updated according to the kind of information needed.

WHY SHOULD WE STUDY BALANCE SHEETS?

Accounting has been called the language of business, and the balance sheet is one of the fundamental accounting documents. Wall Street brokerage firms and investment banks pay millions of dollars annually to financial analysts whose main job is to analyze company financial statements. Banks and other lending institutions train their loan officers to analyze loan applicants' balance sheets. Financial officers of large corporations devote a great deal of time to improving the corporate balance sheets.

The reason people pay so much attention to balance sheets is that balance sheets, together with income statements and other information, enable managers and analysts to learn how a company is doing in many different areas. Chapter 9 of this book focuses on how analysts employ ratios or relationships between balance sheet numbers to compare a company's performance with its own past performance and with other companies in its field. Does the company have a sufficient amount of working capital (current assets less current liabilities)? Is the company a good prospect for a mortgage loan? Should a bond issue be approved? What kind of a return can stockholders hope for on their investment?

Within companies, managers and business owners can learn a lot from balance sheets. Many companies produce balance sheets frequently (once a month, for instance) for their own use, in addition to preparing a formal annual report. By analyzing a succession of balance sheets and income statements, managers and owners can spot both problems and opportunities. Could the company make more profitable use of its assets? Does inventory turnover indicate the most efficient possible use of inventory in sales? How does the company's administrative expense compare to that of its competition?

For the experienced and well-informed reader, then, the balance sheet can be an immensely useful aid in an analysis of the company's overall financial picture.

EXAMPLES

Balance Sheet Overview

Consider the fictional balance sheet in example 1.1. Take a few moments to become familiar with its components and their locations. Notice that the basic accounting equation is satisfied: The two sides of the statement balance. As you look at the two columns of figures, you might ask yourself questions like:

- How will the levels of assets and liabilities be different for different companies? What is appropriate? For example, why is it acceptable for a supermarket to have a high level of inventory while a manufacturing company may have a lower level of inventory? (Answer: because supermarkets without inventory have no customers, whereas in manufacturing companies high inventories may indicate over-production or poor sales.)
- What problems will a low cash level create?
- What about accounts payable and accounts receivable; how large should they be relative to each other and relative to other balance sheet items?
- What level of long-term debt is appropriate?

The answers to these questions may not be obvious. And indeed there are no set standards or hard-and-fast answers to any of these kinds of questions. Much depends on a company's specific circumstances at a given time. Still, it is by

Example 1.1

XYZ Company
Statement of Financial Condition
As of December 31, 19XX

ASSETS		LIABILITIES AND EQUITY	
Current assets:		Current liabilities:	
Cash	$ 12,500	Accounts payable	$ 33,851
Accounts receivable	45,268	Long-term debt— current portion	2,500
Inventory	77,621		
Prepaid expenses	450	Total current liabilities	36,351
Total current assets	135,839	Long-term debt	77,500
Land and buildings (net of depreciation)	54,585	Total liabilities	113,851
		Owners' equity:	
		Owners' capital	25,000
Equipment	3,325	Retained earnings	54,898
		Total equity	79,898
		Total liabilities	
Total assets	$193,749	and equity	$193,749

---

asking questions that you will gradually develop an ability to understand and interpret balance sheets.

Balance Sheet Comparison

Let us look at another simple example. You are a bank loan officer. Your task is to approve a $50,000 loan to either Alpha Company Inc. or Beta Manufacturing Company to expand existing operations. Both are small manufacturers. Alpha manufactures stick-on labels; Beta specializes in a line of point-of-purchase fad accessories. On the basis of the information provided, which company would you approve, and why?

Example 1.2 shows the Alpha and Beta balance sheets. For loan analysis purposes, take a look at three aspects:

1. Asset composition and quality: What is owned?
2. Current assets versus current liabilities; this comparison can reveal short-term problems.
3. Ownership of the assets; that is, proportion of owners' equity to total assets.

Alpha Company Inc. has sufficient value in land, buildings, and equipment to use these assets as collateral for a loan. It has an adequate amount of cash, and accounts receivable do not seem to be too high (which would indicate successful collection of amounts due the company). Alpha's current assets are far in excess of current liabilities, so we can assume that there will be no short-term problems that could drain the assets of the company. Alpha's owners own roughly 44 percent of the company. With this much at stake, they are less likely to do risky things with the company (and the loan!).

Beta Manufacturing Company is not a very healthy company. Its assets consist primarily of inventories and accounts receivable. Accounts receivable that low relative to the total value of the assets may be a sign of poor sales. And inventories that large, especially in a company that produces fad items, may indicate both overproduction and lack of sales. When fads wane, demand can cease almost overnight; Beta could be left holding a large unsalable inventory. Further, if we remove inventory from current assets, we are left with $39,313, which is much lower than current liabilities. This could suggest payment problems in the offing. Finally, the owners of Beta have only 21 percent equity. Compared to Alpha, Beta seems a poorer loan prospect.

Let me reemphasize here, though, that interpretation of financial statements relies on knowledge, experience, common sense, and information from many sources. For example,

Example 1.2

Alpha Company Inc.
Statement of Financial Condition
As of December 31, 19XX

ASSETS		LIABILITIES AND EQUITY	
Current assets:		Current liabilities:	
Cash	$ 22,500	Accounts payable	$ 63,851
Accounts		Long-term debt—	
receivable	65,268	current portion	2,500
Inventory	57,621		
Prepaid		Total current	
expenses	450	liabilities	66,351
Total current		Long-term debt	57,500
assets	145,839		
		Total liabilities	123,851
Land and		Owners' equity:	
buildings (net of		Owners' capital	37,000
depreciation)	48,585		
Equipment	24,892	Retained earnings	58,465
		Total equity	95,465
		Total liabilities	
Total assets	$219,316	and equity	$219,316

---

how would our loan analysis have changed if we knew that
Alpha was the defendant in a $100,000 lawsuit that it would
probably lose, while Beta had just signed a contract to provide
another company with $100,000 per year of its products?

SUMMARY

Balance sheets, income statements, equity statements, and
other information make up a company's financial statements.
A balance sheet is a record of the assets, liabilities, and equity

Example 1.2 (continued)

Beta Manufacturing Company
Statement of Financial Condition
As of December 31, 19XX

ASSETS		LIABILITIES AND EQUITY	
Current assets:		Current liabilities:	
Cash	$ 2,500	Accounts payable	$ 82,827
Accounts receivable	36,813	Long-term debt— current portion	12,500
Inventory	117,621		
Total current assets	156,934	Total current liabilities	95,327
		Long-term debt	77,500
		Total liabilities	172,827
Land and buildings (net of depreciation)	54,585	Owners' equity:	
Equipment	6,729	Owners' capital	25,000
		Retained earnings	20,421
		Total equity	45,421
Total assets	$218,248	Total liabilities and equity	$218,248

---

of a business as of a particular date. It may also be referred to as a statement of financial condition or a statement of financial position.

Assets are what a business owns. Liabilities are what a business owes to nonowners. Equity, or what a business owes to owners, is equal to the value of assets minus liabilities.

An income statement shows profit or loss resulting from operations over the course of a fiscal period, usually a year. If income exceeds expenses, the company shows a profit; if expenses exceed income, the company experiences a loss. The income statement, the balance sheet, and the equity statement together form a coherent history of the business enterprise.

Footnotes and other information are important parts of a company's formal financial statements.

Analysis of income statement figures can help managers, investors, and other interested people assess the relative strengths and weaknesses of companies.

PART

II

Assets

C H A P T E R

2   Cash

On a typical balance sheet cash is the item listed first under current assets, because cash is the most *liquid* of all assets. Cash is readily accepted by everyone. No further conversion is necessary. No valuation is necessary. Think of "liquidity" as a company's ability to convert assets to cash. Companies pay debts by means of cash transfers. Thus, the amount of cash available to a company (together with the ease with which other assets may be converted to cash by sale) determines the company's ability to pay its debts.

The general acceptability of cash makes it an extremely valuable asset. It also means, as this chapter will detail, that companies must carefully control the uses of their cash on several different planes. Companies should chart general movements of cash and changes in cash position from month to month through cash flow statements. And on a hands-on level, organizations of every size and type must institute systems and procedures to safeguard cash against theft or loss.

WHAT IS CASH?

The term *cash* refers, of course, to currency—coin and paper money. In business cash also includes balances in unrestricted checking accounts; negotiable instruments such as checks, drafts, and money orders that are in the company's possession at the time of reporting; petty cash funds (see discussion below); and supplies of change for cash registers.

Business financial reports may also list "cash equivalents." These are somewhat less liquid (less immediately available for use) and include such instruments as certificates of deposit (CDs), Treasury bills, money market funds, and so on.

Many companies have one more form of cash: unavailable cash, or cash deposits that cannot be used for current operations for one reason or another. Examples include employee expense advances (prepaid expenses); deposits with utility companies, even though they will eventually be refunded; minimum or compensating loan balances that are required to be maintained under a bank loan agreement; CD amounts that carry penalties for conversion to cash; and certain foreign bank deposits that cannot be used outside the countries in which they are deposited. All these amounts qualify as company assets, but they should not be listed as cash for reporting purposes because they are not readily available for use.

The valuation of cash is straightforward compared to the valuation of some other assets. (For example, as we'll see later, valuation of inventories may be at "cost" or "market," and the book values of fixed assets depend on the depreciation procedures used.) Cash and bank balances in U.S. depositories are valued simply at the face value printed on U.S. dollars. Checks against U.S. banks, too, are immediately negotiable at their face value. The values of foreign currency, checks, and balances in foreign depositories, however, are subject to daily fluctuations in dollar exchange rates. They must be converted to U.S. dollars at the exchange rate prevailing as of the balance sheet date.

WHAT IS CASH FLOW?

Cash flow statements, usually compiled once a month, detail the sources and uses of cash within an organization. Cash flow is important because it helps reveal how a company is utilizing its most liquid asset. Cash flow statements follow the general format:

Beginning cash balance + Sources of cash − Uses of cash = Ending cash balance

(See example 2.4 later in the chapter.)

Visualize a cash account as a box containing an amount of cash. Several pipes enter one side of the box; another group of pipes exits the other side. The entering pipes are sources of cash, the exiting pipes are uses of cash. In this image, the volume of cash that moves through the box during the month is the total cash flow. The net change in cash is the difference between the beginning and ending cash balances.

By observing the patterns of cash flow in a succession of cash flow statements, a company owner or manager can form a clear picture of where cash is coming from and where it is going—and can draw conclusions, perhaps, about changes that need to be made to improve the company's cash flow situation. Some typical sources and uses of cash include the following (and there are many others). As you glance down these lists, you may want to consider how each type of item affects cash flow in a company.

Sources of cash	Uses of cash
Cash sales	Payments to suppliers
Payment of accounts receivable	Payroll net to employees
Sale of assets	Payroll taxes and withholdings
Loan proceeds	Tax payments
Proceeds from sale of stock	Purchase of assets or inventory
	Loan payments
	Repurchase of stock

In addition to statements of cash flow, companies also compile working capital statements. Working capital is defined as the dollar value of total current assets minus total current liabilities. Also referred to as net working capital or net current assets, it is an important measure of liquidity and short-term financial strength. But while working capital is a helpful indicator of the short-term position, a firm with good working capital may still have cash flow problems. All businesses are ultimately concerned with cash flow.

PROTECTION OF CASH ASSETS

Cash is probably the single most important asset a company can possess, and protection of cash is necessary to ensure the survival of a business. Cash is, however, fast-moving and universally attractive. It is easily transported, hard to identify or trace (despite serial numbers printed on paper currency), and easy to convert to any kind of goods or services. For these reasons, every company must devise ways to protect cash—and prevention of problems before they occur is the watchword. Let's look at a few ways in which companies can protect cash assets.

Bonding

A bond is an insurance policy that protects a company from financial losses due to employee theft or errors beyond management's control. Many company managers or owners take the preventive step of seeing that all individuals who handle cash are bonded by name and in the appropriate amount. Companies should also bond all sensitive positions as such. It is often worthwhile, too, to review the physical arrangement of the cash handling area(s) with the company's insurance broker.

Separation of Functions

Different cash functions—receipts, disbursements, petty cash, and reconciliation of accounts—should be controlled by different people within a business. This way, no one person can control the cash flow or financial statements.

Monitoring

An unnoticed cash leakage, whether through lost receipts or through unauthorized withdrawals, can do severe damage or even cause a business to run out of cash. Monitoring all personnel who handle cash as they do their jobs is perhaps the only certain way of ensuring protection. This is impractical, however, in most companies of any size.

Receipts Control

Every company needs systems to ensure that cash received gets safely to the depository. Loss of currency is a major hazard, although checks and other forms of payment can also be lost if not carefully controlled. Companies must provide for cash to be securely received, as well as setting up internal methods to prevent the disappearance of cash once it is received.

Currency Receipts

The modern supermarket is a good example of a business equipped with a system to control huge amounts of currency changing hands through hundreds or thousands of transactions every day. At the supermarket cash register, the prices of all items are either electronically read from the *Universal Product Codes* (bar codes) on packages or manually keyed into the register. The cashier gives a tape to the customer, and a duplicate tape remains locked inside the register. Usually a visual display attached to the register shows the amount of each item sold, so that it can be seen and checked by the customer—and by the manager. Periodically, the store reconciles the amount of cash in the register with the record of sales, taking into account adjustments for the change fund, bottle credits, and so forth. To the extent practical, cashiers should be held responsible for any discrepancies in the currency receipts. As you can see, this system incorporates multiple safeguards against any cash shrinkage at the hands of employees.

Collections on Accounts Receivable

Monies received as payments on accounts receivable may be paid by the customer either in person or by mail. In either case, separation of functions will help guard against employees siphoning off received cash somewhere between the customer and the company bank account.

When a customer pays in person, the employee dealing with the customer should prepare a receipt, give the original to the customer, and send a copy to the company cashier along with the money. Another copy of the receipt goes to accounts receivable for posting to the customer's account.

Many companies, including department stores, mail-order businesses, and utility companies, receive large volumes of currency by mail. These companies can help prevent loss of cash by setting up teams of two people working together to open the envelopes and record the receipts. This pairing system has been shown to help promote the truthful recording of amounts received. Once recorded, the cash goes to the cashier along with a receipts list. All currency received should be deposited "intact"—down to the last penny. When and if the mode of cash receipt changes, the company should review its receipts control system to determine if the method of recording used should also change. Using a rubber endorsement stamp on checks both speeds up the processing of checks received and adds a measure of security. For example:

XYZ Corporation

Account no. 123-456-78

For deposit only.

A copy of each receipts list sent to the cashier should also go to accounts receivable, to be posted to the customers' accounts. Accounts receivable generates the monthly statements to customers, which should then be deposited directly in a U.S. Post Office depository, not routed through the company mail room. By the same token, customer letters inquiring about charges and payments should go directly to accounts receivable, also bypassing the mail room. The goal of these separation-of-functions procedures is to eliminate any temptation to interfere with the mail. For example, if Ms. X in the cash receipts department were trying to steal cash from the firm, she might be aware that customer letters complaining about overbilling could reveal her scheme; if she had access to the mail, she could try to delay discovery by intercepting and destroying any such letters. It is prudent to forestall problems by minimizing the number of people who handle customer correspondence.

Disbursements Control

Whereas in receipts control the primary challenge is to get currency safely into the depository, the aim of disbursements control is to prevent monies from leaving company accounts in unauthorized ways. Here, control of currency as such is not the issue so much as control of checks, drafts, electronic transfers, and other means of withdrawal.

Check-Writing Procedures

It is easy to remove company cash from a depository: all one needs is a company check. By definition, a *check* requests a depository to give money to the payee, who can then either deposit the check amount or negotiate the check for currency. It is therefore important that every company have a means of controlling its check stock so that only those employees authorized to prepare checks have access to them. Once again, separation of functions is the key; in a typical system, one person approves a bill for payment, a second prepares the check, and a third signs the check.

One effective control mechanism is the *voucher* system. Each invoice received is recorded on a standard voucher form (figure 2.1), to which the invoice is attached. A clerk prepares the voucher and makes the distribution to the proper account(s). Another person checks and initials the voucher, which is then filed by payment date. When the payment date arrives, a clerk prepares the check, taking the appropriate discount (see chapter 6) if called for. Then the authorized check signer reviews the check with the voucher and attached documentation before signing. The check signer also supervises the mailing to avoid the possibility that the check might be removed from the mail room. Returned checks should be routed to someone outside this procedure stream.

Another control system calls for *dual signatures* on all checks paid; that is, two individuals must sign every check before it is negotiable. This system should be used with caution, however. Each signator is supposed to examine the supporting documents and then sign the check if everything is in order, but procedures can become lax over time. Prob-

Vendor Name ———————	Voucher
Address ———————	#6793

Purchase Order No.	Payment
Date Received	Date
Terms	

Account Debited			Approvals
030	Inventories	$ ———————	
040	Fixed Assets	———————	Purchasing Agent
014	Petty Cash	———————	
029	Payroll Taxes	———————	Voucher Super.
028	Employee Withholds	———————	
——	———————	———————	Check Writer
——	———————	———————	
——	———————	———————	
——	———————	———————	
021	Accounts Payable Cr.	$	Transfer

Figure 2.1 Voucher

lems can arise if both cosigners do not review the documentation, each assuming that the other has done so. In general, it works better to use single-signature checks up to a certain amount and to require two signatures for checks above that amount. The reason is that both signators are more likely to review the documentation if the amount is sufficiently large.

Multiple Accounts

Disbursements control presents special challenges when a company has more than one checking account, particularly when there is a branch office in another city. Special procedures are required to monitor the movement of funds between the accounts. An alert manager or owner should discuss with the firm's outside accountant or financial consultant how to prevent any misuse of multiple accounts.

For example, if funds are transferred between accounts, the withdrawal from one account should show up at the same time as the deposit in the other. The company should investigate any delay between withdrawal and deposit to be sure that the person making the withdrawal has not temporarily borrowed funds without authorization. Conversely, a deposit to one account in a fiscal period with a withdrawal shown on another account in the next period may be a sign of *kiting*— that is, an effort to make one account temporarily reflect more cash than the company actually has.

Bank Reconciliation

The company bank account is a record of cash flow. It reflects both receipts and disbursements of company funds. The bank statement should be reconciled with company cash records as soon as the statement arrives each month.

Here, once again, separation of functions is an excellent way to prevent any manipulation of the figures. Someone other than receipts or disbursements personnel should reconcile the company's bank statement. In some cases, statements go directly to an outside firm that keeps the books for the company. The person doing the reconciling, whether inside or outside the company, returns to the initial record of receipts and checks that record against the bank statement for amount and timeliness of arrival. He or she also reviews the endorsements on the company's returned disbursement checks to be sure that all checks paid have gone where they were supposed to go. Finally, the reconciler makes sure that the bank and company balances match. (Examples 2.1 through 2.3, below, relate to this procedure.) Any adjustments required should be "booked"—that is, entered in the company's books.

No._____ Amount $_____

RECEIVED OF PETTY CASH

_____19__

For_____

Charge to_____

_____

_____   _____
Approved by   Received by

Figure 2.2 Petty Cash Voucher

Petty Cash

While it is best to pay all bills by check, it is not practical to write checks for small incidental outlays such as postage due, taxi fares, tips, or tolls. A *petty cash fund* is the mechanism that provides cash for these frequent small disbursements.

To initiate the petty cash fund, a company names a petty cashier and gives the cashier a fixed sum of money by check. When a company member requires a reimbursement, he or she prepares and signs a petty cash voucher (see figure 2.2), and the cashier pays the money from the fund. The total of vouchers and remaining cash in the fund should always equal the initial amount deposited. When cash in the fund is low, the petty cashier surrenders vouchers with a request for a replenishment check in the total amount of the surrendered vouchers. The surrendered vouchers are then posted to the appropriate company or client accounts.

A company should keep a watchful eye on its petty cash fund. Periodic reviews will help avoid tying up too much cash (as indicated by infrequent replenishment or only partial use) or not having a large enough fund (indicated by too-frequent requests for replenishment).

A Note for Small Businesses

A small company may not have a staff large enough to allow for the full range of separations of functions outlined above. Still, separation of functions should be carried out to the greatest extent possible. Consider the receipts control area, for instance. If Fred, of Fred's Bookstore, does not have complete faith in his employees' integrity, he may wish to record personally all cash received. Then his office assistant can enter receipts in the account books. This way, Fred's own record serves as a means of tracing and double-checking cash amounts.

When Fred's Bookstore pays its bills, it may use a simple payment control system such as the three-part voucher check (figure 2.3). The first copy, which is the check, goes to the payee. Fred files the second copy by check number, attaching the invoice and any other supporting documents. He uses the third copy for expense recording and analysis and files this copy under the category of expenditure, such as wages, supplies, or auto expense.

EXAMPLES

The discussion in this chapter has moved from the general (the importance of cash and the meaning of cash flow) to the particular (cash protection systems and procedures). In the examples that follow, we'll go in the opposite direction: from a particular procedure to analysis of a hypothetical general situation.

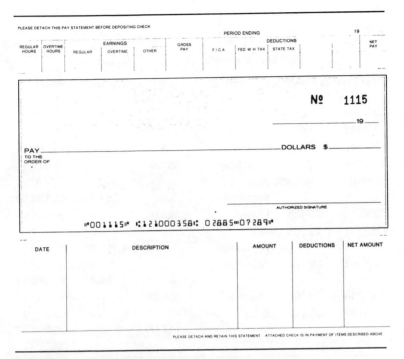

Figure 2.3   Voucher Check

Bank Account Reconciliation

Regular reconciliation of company records with bank records is critical. In an ideal world, the bank statement's balance as of the statement date would match the balance shown in the company checkbook. Because of timing differences (and errors), however, this almost never happens. Hence the need to "reconcile" the discrepancies between the two sets of figures. If approached logically, the reconciliation procedure is simple.

Use two-column accounting ledger paper. At the top of one column, write the checkbook balance. At the top of the other, write the balance from the bank statement. Under the checkbook balance, record all debits and credits that appear on the

Example 2.1

Checkbook Register for Your Company

Transaction	Date	Description	Withdrawal	Deposit	Balance
Previous balance					18,451.21
CK#242	2-Jun	Inventory	2,534.49		15,916.72
CK#243	4-Jun	Postage	18.57		15,898.15
CK#244	4-Jun	Inventory	986.00		14,912.15
Deposit	10-Jun	A/R payments		1,254.79	16,166.94
CK#245	15-Jun	Payroll	5,525.00		10,641.94
Deposit	23-Jun	A/R payments		4,518.23	15,160.17
Deposit	29-Jun	Sales for June		5,789.80	20,949.97
CK#246	30-Jun	Supplies	250.00		20,699.97
CK#247	30-Jun	Rent expense	1,145.00		19,554.97

---

bank statement but not in the checkbook. Under the bank balance, record all deposits and checks that appear in the checkbook but do not appear on the bank statement. After adding both columns down, you should have identical balances. If not, look for simple addition and recording errors; for example, check number 2483 might be recorded in the checkbook as $350 and on the bank statement as $305.

Suppose that in May of 19XX, your checkbook and bank statements balance. Your check register and bank statement may resemble examples 2.1 and 2.2. Your bank reconciliation might look like example 2.3.

After reconciliation, adjustments to the checkbook should be entered in the check register and posted to any necessary accounts.

Example 2.2

Friendly Bank and Trust Company
Your Company
Statement of Account

1-Jun	Beginning balance	18,451.21
	Deposits	
11-Jun	Deposit	1,254.79
23-Jun	Deposit	4,518.23
	Total deposits	5,773.02
	Withdrawals	
4-Jun	Check #242	2,534.49
6-Jun	Check #244	986.00
9-Jun	Check #243	18.57
15-Jun	Service charge	10.00
15-Jun	Check #245	5,525.00
	Total withdrawals	9,074.06
	Ending balance	15,150.17

Example 2.3

Account Reconciliation for June 19XX

Checkbook ending		Statement balance	15,150.17
balance	19,554.97		
Service charge	−10.00	Check# 246	−250.00
		Check# 247	−1,145.00
		Deposit in transit	5,789.80
Total	19,544.97	Total	19,544.97

Sources and Uses of Cash

A company compiles a cash flow statement by analyzing its cash account. Example 2.4 shows a very abbreviated cash

Example 2.4

Your Company
Cash Flow Statement
For Month Ending June 30, 19XX

Beginning cash balance		$18,451.21
Sources of funds:		
Cash sales	$5,789.80	
Accounts receivable payments	5,773.02	
Net funds supplied from operations		11,562.82
Total funds available		30,014.03
Uses of funds:		
Inventory expense	3,520.49	
Payroll expense	5,525.00	
Supplies expense	250.00	
Rent expense	1,145.00	
Postage expense	18.57	
Net uses of funds		10,459.06
Ending balance		$19,554.97
Net change in cash for June		$ 1,103.76

---

flow statement based on the check register from example 2.1 above.

(For the sake of clarity, these examples are highly condensed and simplified. In an actual situation, you would utilize much fuller information and additional financial statements.)

While a full-scale analysis of sources and uses of funds may be quite complicated, the basic information about cash flow can often be used to assess the health of an enterprise. Imagine that you are a partner in Delta Enterprises Inc. You have just received the company balance sheet, example 2.5, which includes the current year and the preceding year for comparison purposes. As you read the figures, think about the sources and uses of cash.

Regarding sources, note that the company has been able to increase its long-term loan in the current year. On the other hand, note that accounts payable have doubled, indicating that Delta does not seem to be paying its bills. And values of land, buildings, and equipment have fallen dramatically; this could indicate the sale of assets, but if so, what happened to the proceeds of the sale? Owners' equity has also plummeted, but again, what has happened to that equity? You might begin to wonder if Delta's cash funds are being mismanaged.

Example 2.6 is a table of sources and uses of funds at Delta. This table seems to confirm your suspicions. In fact, it appears that your fellow partners may have begun liquidating the company. Clearly, what is going on does not reflect a strategy decision, because the company would not have received approval for a new bank loan if liquidation was on its agenda. This *looks* like fraud. Indeed, without more information fraud looks like the most likely answer to the question, "Where has all the money gone?"

SUMMARY

Cash is the most liquid of all assets, and the amount of cash available to a company determines the company's liquidity, or ability to meet its current obligations. The term cash refers to currency and instruments readily convertible to currency.

Cash flow statements detail the sources and uses of cash within an organization. Cash flow helps reveal how a company is utilizing its cash. Statements of working capital

Example 2.5

Delta Enterprises Inc.
Statement of Financial Condition
As of December 31, 19X2 and 19X1

ASSETS	19X2	19X1	LIABILITIES AND EQUITY	19X2	19X1
Current assets:			Current liabilities:		
Cash	$ 1,500	$ 18,250	Accounts payable	$ 72,756	$ 35,497
Accounts receivable	43,765	72,828	Long-term debt— current portion	24,000	12,000
Inventory	47,691	73,954			
Prepaid expenses	0	1,700	Total current liabilities	96,756	47,497
			Long-term debt	73,000	60,000
Total current assets	92,956	166,732	Total liabilities	169,756	107,497
Land and buildings (net of depreciation)	54,585	77,900	Owners' equity:		
			Owners' capital	100,000	100,000
Equipment	26,729	59,871	Retained earnings	-95,486	97,006
			Total equity	4,514	197,006
Total assets	$174,270	$304,503	Total liabilities and equity	$174,270	$304,503

Example 2.6

Delta Enterprises
Sources and Uses of Funds Summary
Year Ending December 31, 19X2

Sources of funds:

Reduction of accounts receivable—net	$ 29,063	
Reduction of inventory—net	26,263	
Sale of land and buildings	23,315	
Sale of equipment	33,142	
Decrease in prepaid expenses	1,700	
Increase in accounts payable	37,259	
Net sources of funds		$175,742

Uses of funds:

Reduction of retained earnings	192,492
Reduction in cash	$16,750

(current assets less current liabilities) also help indicate
short-term liquidity and financial strength.

Protection of cash is vital to ensure the survival of a
business. In both receipts and disbursements, systems and
procedures based on separation of functions help prevent
manipulation of cash by individuals in the company. Inde-
pendent reconciliation of company cash accounts are wise
forms of insurance against cash loss. A petty cash fund is a
practical way to provide for small outlays. While small businesses may not be able to institute the elaborate systems used
in larger enterprises, cash control is important even in smaller
companies.

3 Receivables

Receivables are claims for sums of money owed to a business by others. While not as liquid as cash, receivables constitute current assets that have value for the company. Like cash, receivables demand careful management.

WHAT ARE RECEIVABLES?

The *receivables*, or accounts receivable, line on a balance sheet includes all amounts owed to the company by others at the time of reporting. The overwhelming preponderance of monies shown as receivables are trade receivables, or amounts owed in payment for the goods or services the company sells to its customers. The receivables figure, therefore, reflects the fact that the business has extended credit of one kind or another to its customers. Whether those customers are individuals, retail establishments, wholesalers, or other business, industrial, or professional organizations, the company has allowed them the privilege of buying goods or services without paying for them until some later date.

A company grants credit to customers because its management believes that the availability of credit will increase sales and profit. And indeed most of us, as individuals, have had the experience of buying something because credit was available, although we might not have bought that same thing if we had had to pay cash immediately. Similarly, corporate and other customers depend on credit for innumerable kinds of transactions. So there are strong positive reasons for a company to use receivables.

At the same time, receivables can be a source of problems. The personnel and paperwork involved in managing large numbers of credit accounts are costly; it is incumbent upon a business to select credit customers prudently and analyze carefully what types of credit it will grant. Also, because sales are not in cash, payment may occur late or not at all. Cash flow problems can result. Finally, as we'll discuss below, financial analysts regard receivables as an asset that in some cases may not be worth its face value because of the possibility of future nonpayment.

Let's take a closer look at credit issues: types of credit, the decision to grant credit, some problems with credit, and some of the ways companies analyze receivables and compute allowances for possible losses.

TYPES OF CREDIT

One of the first questions a business must ask is what type of credit will best serve its purposes. Since many customers will make a purchase if allowed a manageable payment schedule, many businesses generate sales by setting up an in-house credit system, whether informal or formal.

An alternative is acceptance of outside credit cards, as discussed later in this chapter.

Informal In-House Credit

Informal in-house credit is typical of small retail establishments where the proprietors know their customers. At Smith's Drugstore, for example, Mrs. Smith opens up an account for a customer and notes all sales by hand on her customer's account card. She and the customer agree orally about when bills will be mailed, how long the customer has to pay them, and so on. Mrs. Smith now sometimes charges interest for overdue accounts. (Some small stores have traditionally added routine charges to accounts for the privilege of buying on credit; it is illegal, however, to do this surreptitiously.) But Mrs. Smith could run into difficulties if her account cards were lost or disputed. If this happened, she might have no recourse but to take the loss herself.

Formal In-House Credit

Formal in-house credit arrangements are widespread. The *credit terms* or stipulations of these arrangements are carefully spelled out and published. Formal in-house credit can exist in virtually any type of company. Well-known examples of businesses that issue their own credit cards are department stores, such as Sears, J. C. Penney, and Bloomingdale's, and fuel companies, such as Texaco, Gulf, and the like. Before deciding to issue credit, each such company must establish whether the volume of business generated will compensate for the cost of maintaining credit accounts. Judgments as to individual customers' creditworthiness represent another area of decision making, as discussed below.

Installment sales represent a special type of formal in-house credit. In an installment plan, customers make partial payments on a regular schedule until the whole purchase price is paid. Usually the seller adds an interest charge to the cash price—the rate and total amount of interest depending on the amount of the purchase and the number of monthly payments. In a *conditional sale* contract, the title to the goods does not pass to the consumer until the whole contract is fulfilled; that is, until all the payments are made. Cost-of-credit statutes now frequently require that a preliminary statement to the purchaser explain clearly the interest rate, the difference between the cash price and the total of the installments plus interest, and the terms under which the consumer may pay off the debt early.

GRANTING CREDIT

The decision to grant credit should not be taken lightly. It is easier to grant credit than to revoke it if problems develop.

Every credit-granting organization must establish a basis for granting or denying credit applications. If other businesses are applying for credit, bank references, previous credit record, financial statements, and tax returns can provide the necessary information. Individual consumers, however, are unlikely to be able to provide personal balance sheets, and credit checks are often necessary. Some companies subscribe to credit bureaus, which collect credit data about individuals (and companies) and make the data available to subscribers. But credit bureau reports can be flawed. By statute the consumer has the right to inspect his or her file and to request correction of disputed elements.

Whatever the type of customer, a business must set and adhere to firm and fair criteria for rating the information collected and making its final decision. For example, a company may use a formula, either self-devised or purchased, that quantifies a customer's credit history along with many other factors. The company may decide that when all the pertinent figures have been plugged into the formula, an arbitrary score—say, 80 percent or higher—will qualify a customer for credit; a score below 80 percent will not. This kind of system creates a rational framework for decision making and provides a plausible explanation for the issuance or denial of credit in each case.

PROBLEMS WITH ISSUING CREDIT

While it can boost sales and profits, issuing credit inevitably raises problems. The value of receivables as a company asset depends upon customers' *ability* and *willingness* to pay.

For our purposes here, there are two types of customers: those who will pay and those who will not. Credit criteria should, therefore, examine both ability and willingness to pay. The dilemma is that if the criteria are set too high, a company loses potential customers; if the criteria are too lax, there is more chance of loss from noncollection of receivables.

For example, if we look at the total potential customer base and rank all the customers by scores according to a creditworthiness formula, we may find a few with scores of 100 percent and many more in the 90, 80, and 70 percent ranges (see figure 3.1). It seems simple to draw the credit eligibility cutoff line at, say, 80 percent. But some of those selected for credit according to this criterion may never pay; in the diagram these are labeled as **B** customers. This scoring system, like any arbitrary selection system, allows some individuals or companies to slip through the screening process and show up only when nonpayment occurs.

Perhaps more important, there are customers who score lower than 80 percent but who would buy and pay promptly if given the opportunity—**A** customers in the diagram. The company would benefit from doing business with these customers if they could be identified.

Credit Rating

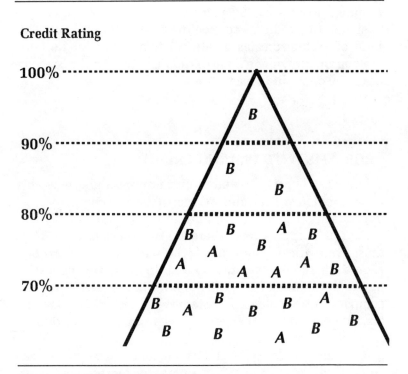

Figure 3.1 The Credit Triangle

In view of these uncertainties, the company may decide to take a calculated risk and accept a lower rating, perhaps 70 percent. Note that in this group there are still more As than Bs; that is, more payers than nonpayers. By monitoring purchases and payments over time, the company can evaluate its lower cutoff score and readjust it if necessary. The judicious raising or lowering of the cutoff score will eventually give the company the desired mixture of customers and a manageable rate of noncollection loss.

Billing and Collection Policies

A crucial element of the decision to grant credit is the establishment of clear procedures for billing and collection. An organization of any size should separate billing and collection functions, because these functions require different skills.

It is important that the date of every receipt be recorded accurately. As detailed in chapter 2, separation of functions should prevail throughout the processing of cash receipts. Once a payment date is recorded, a copy of the receipt goes to accounts receivable for posting; since accounts receivable personnel have no access to cash, the receipt and cash go to the company cashier. The accounts receivable department records the amount of the receipt, the invoices to which the cash relates, and the amount of any applicable discount (see *Allowing Discounts*, below). If the customer has taken the discount after the allowed date, receivables personnel contact the customer about discount terms.

The effectiveness of a company's collection effort is a key factor in increasing profits. The company promptly prepares the *invoice*—the document showing what was delivered, when it was delivered, and the amount due. The invoice accompanies the merchandise or service when delivered. Later, the company sends out month-end statements and includes in the printed credit terms some penalty for late payment (interest) or inducement for prompt payment (discount). Within a reasonable time after the statement date, or at least on the next statement, the company recontacts all unpaid accounts. When the oldest item on a statement goes beyond a specified number of days, accounts receivable personnel make a phone call or write a letter demanding payment. After another period of time, a letter is sent indicating that the account will be turned over to a collection agency.

Before this stage, accounts receivable should consult with the sales department to learn if special circumstances exist. The overall collection policy requires thought by management as to what to do, who should do it, and when. A well-thought-out, fair, and (if needed) forceful course of action will reduce losses from noncollection.

Charging Interest

Charging interest on receivables after a predetermined length of time is a way for a company to (1) compensate for its own reduction in available cash (and possibly its need to borrow cash while awaiting receivables), and (2) enhance the buyers' willingness to pay promptly.

Essentially, by extending credit a company is allowing customers to use company monies for a certain period of time. Why do businesses bankroll customers, even for a short time? Many organizations find that the profit outweighs the costs of deferred receipts and/or noncollection losses. For example, suppose a company, by the use of credit, were to increase sales by $100,000 and gross profit by $30,000. If 10 percent of the accounts were paid one month late and the company had to replace that missing $10,000 each month by borrowing at 12 percent annual interest (an interest cost of $12,000 over the course of the year), and if $500 remained uncollectible, there would still be a net profit increase of $17,500.

A company may, however, decide to reduce the interest loss by adding to its credit terms a phrase such as "All balances over 30 days will be charged interest at 12 percent per annum," or "Interest will be charged on balances over 30 days up to $1,500 at 1.5 percent per month and on amounts above $1,500 at 1 percent per month." These kinds of terms tend to make collections more certain, because the interest rate charged often exceeds that of other forms of borrowing. In setting terms, companies take into account current economic conditions as well as trade practice (trade custom).

Allowing Discounts

Another way to motivate buyers to pay promptly is to offer *cash discounts*. The company may specify credit terms as, for example, "2/30; n/60." This means that if an invoice is paid within 30 days of purchase or delivery, the purchaser may deduct 2 percent from the purchase price. After 30 days, the full, or "net," invoice price is due, and it is payable 60 days from the purchase or delivery date. Trade practice is the company's guide as to whether to use the purchase or the delivery date. Under these terms, on a $1,500 purchase made on January 22 a payment of $1,470 would be due by February 22, or the whole $1,500 by March 24. (Businesses often use an assumed 30-day month and consider the period from one date to the same date the next month as 30 days, except in February, when they assume 28 or 29 days.)

There may also be a two-phase discount structure. For instance, the terms might be stated as "2/30; 1/60; n/90," meaning that there is a 2 percent discount on the invoice price if paid within 30 days, or 1 percent if paid within 60 days; full invoice price is due in 90 days.

For the purchaser, a discount amounts to the equivalent of a very good investment. For example, if a buyer pays a 2/30 invoice within 30 days, the effect is the same as earning a 24 percent annual rate on an investment. To see how this works, assume a purchase of $1,000 at 2/30. The 30-day discount is $20. To earn $20 in a month, $1,000 would have to be invested at an annual rate of 24 percent. This kind of discount, then, is a decided inducement for the customer to pay bills within the discount period. And to collect receivables early in order to lessen the risk of loss is a powerful inducement for companies to extend cash discount terms.

Cash Flow Problems

A company can develop a cash flow problem as a result of granting credit, because granting credit allows receivables to mount up while invoices that must be paid in cash keep coming in. But there are methods of alleviating this problem. If a business has a large amount of receivables but little cash, it can use its receivables to secure cash.

One way to do this is to sell the receivables outright at a discounted rate to a bank or other lending institution. The bank, in this example, notifies the company's credit customers that it has purchased the company's receivables and that the customers should make payments to it rather than to the company. Any payments sent to the company are forwarded to the bank. If the bank purchases the receivables and agrees not to return them to the company, the transaction is said to be "without recourse." The bank alone risks the loss from nonpayment. If the bank can eventually return any unpaid items, the transaction is said to be "with recourse."

Receivables can also be used as collateral; that is, they can be given to a lending institution as security for a loan. Most businesses prefer that their customers not know that they are borrowing against receivables. When a business has given its receivables as collateral, it often keeps the receivables records, mails the statements, and collects the monies paid on account. Most lending institutions will comply with this arrangement so long as their loans are protected. Under the usual agreement, the company routinely collects the money and forwards to the lender all payments received, while giving the lender enough additional unpaid receivables to secure the loan.

RECOGNIZING LOSSES FROM RECEIVABLES

The billing and collection policy of a company should spell out not only when billing will occur and what the terms of credit are but what the collection procedure is—that is, when collection letters or agencies will be brought into play. But despite the best-planned policies and efforts, losses do sometimes occur, and a balance sheet must reflect this fact.

As an account receivable becomes older, the chance of collection becomes less. The company must decide when to write off the account or to take the loss due to expected nonpayment. Accountants have two ways of recording the loss: (1) the direct write-off method and (2) the allowance and write-off method.

Direct Write-off Method

The *direct write-off method* is employed when the account is deemed ultimately uncollectible and is charged off to a bad debt account. This method has the disadvantage of recording the sale at the time it was made and the write-off expense at a subsequent time. In so doing, direct write-off violates the basic accounting principle of matching income and its related expense in time.

Allowance and Write-off Method

The *allowance and write-off method* avoids violating the matching principle. Each year the assets side of the balance sheet shows a credit item called "Allowance for Bad Debts" or "Allowance for Doubtful Accounts" and subtracts this from the amount shown as accounts receivable. The net amount is then expected to be collected on accounts receivable. Because it is a credit in the assets section, allowance for bad debts is called a *contra-asset account*—an asset-valuation account with a credit balance that is subtracted from the asset to determine the asset's net worth.

The problem becomes one of determining the amount of this account. A company with a relatively long credit experience can estimate a statistical relationship between its year-end accounts receivable and its expected losses. The easiest formula is to have the balance in the contra-asset account at the end of the period equal to a percentage of the year-end receivables.

A more realistic method to compute the contra-asset amount, however, is to age the accounts receivable, assigning smaller percentages to the newer account balances and greater percentages to the older ones. An "aging schedule of accounts receivable" categorizes accounts receivable according to their ages. For example:

ABC Company
Aging Schedule of Accounts Receivable
June 30, 19X5

	$
Current	72,908
31–60 days	26,723
61–90 days	9,456
Over 90 days	1,144
Total	110,231

This kind of schedule is an informal, in-house document. It gives a more precise picture of the status of receivables than does the total receivables amount ($110,231) and may aid in determining how large the allowance for bad debts should be.

The schedule may be analyzed by percentages:

ABC Company
Aging Schedule of Accounts Receivable
June 30, 19X5

	$	%
Current	72,908	66.14
31–60 days	26,723	24.24
61–90 days	9,456	8.58
Over 90 days	1,144	1.04
Total	110,231	100.00

In this example, 66 percent of receivables are current. The remainder may need some additional collection effort or may ultimately have to be written off.

If the company deems an individual account to be uncollectible, it writes off the amount and charges it to the allowance for bad debts account. Each year after the system is established, charging off accounts deemed uncollectible reduces the beginning balance in the allowance account; at the end of the year, the allowance account is again brought up to the expected loss amount. All additions to bring the allowance account up to the expected loss are charged to the "Bad Debt Expense" account on the debit side of the income statement. Meanwhile, the use of the allowance account has placed the expected loss in the year of the sale and affirmed the accounting principle of matching income with expense.

USING OUTSIDE CREDIT

A widespread means of providing credit is through outside credit cards, such as American Express, MasterCard, VISA, or Discover. The credit card companies promote these cards to both consumers and businesses. By accepting outside credit cards, a retailer or other establishment is indirectly extending credit to the customer.

It is the business's responsibility to check credit card expiration dates and to check cards against a list of stolen or invalid cards. If a card appears on that list, the business is required to confiscate the card and return it to the credit company (for which the business will be paid a fee). Having accepted a customer's credit card in payment for a purchase, the business deposits the completed and signed credit charge slips with its bank. The bank credits the retailer's account, deducting a small percentage as a fee. If the business has taken routine precautions (checking the expiration date, checking the list of bad cards, calling the credit company if the amount is over a certain limit), it will be assured that the amount of the sale less the service fee will be credited unconditionally to its account. That is, if the amount turns out later to be uncollectible, it is the credit card company that will take the loss.

Credit card companies also handle the processes of evaluating customers' creditworthiness, billing consumers, posting charges and payments, charging interest if appropriate, collecting payments, and pursuing late payments. Many businesses find that all these services are well worth the fee deducted by the bank. In addition, by honoring internationally accepted cards a business can serve customers from all over the world without having to check on their creditworthiness case by case. All in all, acceptance of outside credit can increase sales and profits with a minimum of effort on the part of the business.

EXAMPLES

Aging Schedule of Accounts Receivable

You are the owner of Friendly Sales Company. It is now March 31, 19XX, time to close the books for the month and examine the financial statements. You have a copy of the February aging schedule of accounts receivable and a report of credit account activity for that month (example 3.1).

Examine the schedule and the report closely. Do you see any problems?

Now, using the figures in example 3.1, construct a new aging schedule of receivables for March. As you compute, remember:

1. All February items are now 30 days older. For example, February currents are March "31–60 days" items, and so on.

2. All March credit purchases are now currently due.

3. All payments apply toward the oldest items first. (This is the general rule businesses use.) As the

Example 3.1

Friendly Sales Company
Aging Schedule of Accounts Receivable
February 28, 19XX

Customer name	Total outstanding	Current	31–60 days	61–90 days	Over 90 days
Tom Jefferson	2,605	1,252	852	501	0
Abe Lincoln	2,035	1,101	934	0	0
Dolly Madison	725	725	0	0	0
Sam Morse	6,626	934	2,131	2,643	918
Eleanor Roosevelt	448	448	0	0	0
Betsy Ross	5,143	1,212	1,650	1,457	824
George Washington	625	625	0	0	0
Martha Washington	1,575	1,164	411	0	0
Totals	19,782	7,461	5,978	4,601	1,742

Account Activity
Month Ending March 31, 19XX

Customer name	Credit purchases	Payments
Tom Jefferson	1,151	1,353
Abe Lincoln	888	1,000
Dolly Madison	700	725
Sam Morse	1,550	0
Eleanor Roosevelt	250	448
Betsy Ross	901	750
George Washington	375	625
Martha Washington	798	411
Totals	6,613	5,312

oldest items are paid off, apply payments to the next oldest, and so on until you reach current items.

4. Every account balance should satisfy the following equation:

Previous balance + Purchase − Payments = Current balance
      19,782   +   6,613 − 5,312   =   21,083

Your new schedule should resemble example 3.2. As you contemplate the new schedule, you may find your earlier instincts confirmed. First, Mr. Morse and Ms. Ross have very delinquent accounts. Second, many of the customers' accounts have substantial noncurrent portions. Perhaps a greater collection effort is necessary. Those that are large and very delinquent certainly need attention. It may be necessary to restrict credit purchases or require only cash purchases from Mr. Morse and/or Ms. Ross. If greater collection efforts fail or renegotiation of the debt is impossible, it may finally be necessary to write off these amounts as a loss.

Allowance for Bad Debts

Look again at Friendly Sales's February 28 aging schedule of accounts (example 3.1). You wish to compile a balance sheet as of February 28. Based on your experience, the following percentages of aged accounts will be uncollectible and will have to be written off:

Current	31–60 days	61–90 days	Over 90 days
1%	3%	8%	20%

On this basis, what should the allowance for uncollectible accounts be?

Your computation should look like this:

7,461(.01) + 5,978(.03)   + 4,601(.08)   + 1,742(.20)   =
    75   +   179   +   368   +   348   = 970

Example 3.2

Friendly Sales Company
Aging Schedule of Accounts Receivable
March 31, 19XX

Customer name	Total outstanding	Current	31–60 days	61–90 days	Over 90 days
Tom Jefferson	2,403	1,151	1,252	0	0
Abe Lincoln	1,923	888	1,035	0	0
Dolly Madison	700	700	0	0	0
Sam Morse	8,176	1,550	934	2,131	3,561
Eleanor Roosevelt	250	250	0	0	0
Betsy Ross	5,294	901	1,212	1,650	1,531
George Washington	375	375	0	0	0
Martha Washington	1,962	798	1,164	0	0
Totals	21,083	6,613	5,597	3,781	5,092

Therefore, the balance sheet will look like this:

Accounts receivable	19,782	
Less allowance for doubtful accounts	970	
Net accounts receivable		18,812

SUMMARY

Receivables, or accounts receivable, are cash amounts owed to a company as of the balance sheet date from the sales of goods or services. These receivables reflect the granting of credit, and companies grant credit in order to increase profits.

Types of credit include informal in-house credit, formal in-house credit, and outside credit issued by credit card companies.

When granting credit, a company must select a firm and fair system of criteria for evaluating customers' eligibility.

Problems with credit include the difficulty of predicting which customers will pay and which will not. Some incentives may induce customers to pay promptly.

Collection procedures should be put in place to ensure proper processing and to minimize loss from noncollections. Charging interest and allowing discounts are mechanisms for encouraging prompt payment. Cash flow problems resulting from unpaid receivables can be alleviated by the sale of receivables or by the use of receivables as collateral for loans.

An allowance for bad debts account is a way to place expected write-offs in the same year as the sales to which they pertain. By "aging" receivables, a company can make a realistic estimate of bad debts for the allowance account.

4   Inventories

Most people over 30 can recall finding a store unexpectedly closed for a day, signs in its windows announcing, "Closed for Inventory." Behind the shuttered facade of the store, employees would be working in pairs, one person calling out quantities of hardware units, shoes, stationery items, or whatever, while a second worker recorded the figures on annual inventory sheets. The word *inventory* comes from the Latin for "to find," and the clerks were literally finding what was on the shelves as it came time to close the store's books for the accounting period.

While this method of inventory counting is rapidly going the way of the vinyl long-playing record, managing inventory remains a vital—and complex—component of every kind of merchandising and manufacturing business.

WHAT ARE INVENTORIES?

Inventories are assets that a business has acquired either for sale or for use in the manufacture of goods for sale. Merchandisers' inventories include finished goods ready for sale or resale. Manufacturers' inventories include raw materials, supplies used in manufacture, and work in process (partly completed goods), as well as finished goods.

What is so complicated about inventory, and why is inventory so important?

The dollar valuation of inventory as a current asset depends on the type of business and the purpose of the valuation. Retail establishments use one system of valuation, manufacturers other systems. Even within a single company, different valuation methods may be applied to different types of inventory. (A note to the company's financial statements may specify what method has been used.) Inventory valuation, of course, enters directly into the calculation of a business's total assets on the balance sheet. Inventory valuation also has an impact on other financial statements, because inventory valuation is part of the computation of the cost of goods sold, and the cost of goods sold directly affects the company's gross profit, income, and taxes.

Quantities of inventory, too, are significant. For every type of inventory there is an optimal quantity for a business to have on hand—enough to meet immediate needs, but not so much as to tie up excessive cash or take up excessive space. Problems with inventory range from overstocking to understocking to loss due to lack of security. Each of these problems can do financial damage to a company.

Careful study and control of inventory, then, is important for company managers. And inventories are important to anyone interested in a particular company or in an industry as a whole. Inventory levels and valuations can indicate economic potential or can provide clues as to possible underlying weaknesses.

TYPES OF INVENTORY

Both merchandising and manufacturing businesses use inventory information to minimize the dollar volume of inventory while allowing sales or manufacturing to proceed smoothly.

Goods for Sale

In a retail or wholesale business, inventories are *finished goods:* completed goods that the business has acquired to sell to customers. Ideally, in each period, the quantity of goods for sale will be exactly the quantity the customers want to buy. Managers try to approach this ideal situation by developing an in-depth knowledge of the stock, the customers' preferences, and the flow of inventory.

No company wants to run short of an item when demand is still high. At the same time, overbuying can result in stocks that become damaged or shopworn or go out of style before they are sold. Every consumer is familiar with merchandisers' efforts to reduce unsold inventory: stratagems such as end-of-season markdowns of seasonal goods or special "warehouse" outlets for leftover and discontinued items.

Inventory information enables a business to ensure that adequate inventory will be on hand while minimizing overstocks. Computerized Universal Product Code (UPC) inventory systems aid substantially in this effort. When an article is sold, the computerized cash register can scan the UPC bars and—in addition to generating data for the sales slip or register tape—deduct the item from inventory and develop a current balance of the item in stock. If the system has a reorder point (a minimum number of units on hand, below which new stock must be purchased), the system generates a listing of items to be ordered and, perhaps, a purchase order. A system that calculates the current balance of inventory after every sale or receipt is called a "perpetual inventory system."

In establishments that do not possess this kind of so-
phisticated computer system, an inventory count at the balance sheet date (or at another date, later reconciled to the
balance sheet date) determines the quantity reflected on the
balance sheet. Some businesses hire outside inventory-taking
firms that use a wand connected to an electronic calculator.
The inventory-taking staffer keys in the quantity of each item;
the wand feeds in descriptions from bar codes on price tags
or shelf labels. Later, perhaps back at the office of the inventory-taking firm, staffers price the items and *extend* the
prices. That is, they multiply the price per unit by the number
of each item. The inventory takers total the extensions to
generate a total inventory count and value.

Finally, some firms count inventory in the traditional way,
using teams of counters, one calling the description and
count, the other recording. The teams may use special three-
part inventory tags. The person doing the recording tears off
one part of the tag after pricing and extending the item; the
company's external auditor checks the second part of the tag;
the third part remains on the item until all inventory questions are resolved.

Merchandise turns over often during the year in the retail
industry. Retailers' big season is Christmas, and most retailers
close their books in January. Therefore, to reduce the number
of items to count (and to prepare space for the spring season),
many retailers hold end-of-the-year sales in January; January
"white sales" are one example.

Materials and Supplies

Raw materials, strictly speaking, are materials that have not
yet entered production, such as iron ore, tree trunks, or wheat.
In this discussion, however, all materials used by a manufacturing firm in the course of production will be included under
the heading of materials and supplies; for example, steel to
make tools, lumber to make cabinets, or white flour to make

bread. In other words, one manufacturing firm's materials often include the finished products of other kinds of manufacturing firms.

Work in Process

Work-in-process inventories, sometimes called partly completed goods or unfinished goods, include materials that are in the process of being turned into goods for sale but are not yet completed as of the end of the fiscal period. When inventorying work in process, inventory takers record not only raw materials but process numbers (part numbers, etc.) and stages of completion of products. In team counting, employees can develop the stage of completion from the factory process sheet.

VALUATION OF INVENTORIES

Valuation of inventories varies according to the type of business or industry doing the valuing.

Goods for Sale

Goods for sale in retail businesses are generally priced at a percentage markup or markdown from cost. This percentage increases or decreases with changes in demand and supply; often the percentage, and the retail price, will fluctuate several times over the life of an item before it is sold. The "retail pricing method" entails keeping a precise record of price movements up and down. At inventory valuation time, a retailer determines the original costs of items by applying the accumulated effects of price movements to the items' current selling prices.

Having ascertained the original cost, retailers designate the inventory valuation as either the historical cost or the current market price, whichever is lower. The purpose of the "cost or market, whichever is lower" valuation is to reduce the inventory to its most conservative figure—that is, to set the dollar worth of year-end inventory as low as possible.

In order to decide whether cost or market value is lower, a retailer may compare the original unit cost of each item to that item's current market price, choose the lowest in each case, and extend all these chosen figures (that is, multiply them by the number of items in inventory) to get a total inventory valuation. A second method is to extend the original unit costs of all inventory items to get a total inventory valuation based on cost, extend the current market prices of all items to get a total inventory valuation based on current market, then use the lower of these two total valuations on the balance sheet. A third method is to apply one of these approaches to some segments of inventory, apply the other to the remaining segments, and total the segments to get the total inventory valuation. Of these three methods, the first is the least costly to carry out, because it requires only one extension for each item. Regardless of which method a retailer uses, any excess price of the inventory on the books over the inventory valuation developed is taken as a cost in the year in which the price went down.

Materials and Supplies

The valuation systems described above apply to businesses whose inventories turn over rapidly and consist solely of finished goods for sale—typically, retail businesses. But in other kinds of businesses and industries, price movements are not so well documented, and inventories may include not only finished goods but materials, supplies, and work in process. Also, in many businesses, end-of-year inventory includes some inventory acquired in previous years, some acquired in the current year. Historical costs of identical items acquired at different times can vary widely.

In these more complicated situations, accountants have developed three basic approaches to valuing end-of-year inventory. Each approach assigns costs to items *sold*—gone from inventory—in order to arrive at a valuation of the inventory remaining at the end of the year.

To understand these approaches, just realize that when items gone from inventory and items remaining in inventory are identical, accountants are not required to allocate to a given item its actual historical cost. For example, suppose Mammoth Widget Corporation begins the year with 30 widgets finished and ready for sale. Of these, 10 cost the company, all told, $3 apiece. The other 20, produced more recently, cost $4 apiece. If Mammoth sells 8 widgets during the year, it can reduce end-of-year inventory by $24, assigning to each unit sold the older $3 cost. Or Mammoth can reduce inventory by $32, assigning the newer $4 cost. Or the company can assign to each widget sold an averaged cost. There are pros and cons to each approach, depending on Mammoth's priorities.

The first method is known as *FIFO:* first-in, first-out. FIFO valuation uses the oldest costs for goods going out of inventory, much as a retailer sells oldest stock first. For Mammoth, FIFO would value each widget sold at $3. In periods of inflation, older costs are generally lower. The effect of FIFO, therefore, is generally to raise the value of remaining inventory. This effectively lowers the "cost of goods sold" figure (see example 4.3 below), which raises profits. On the other hand, the FIFO method often fails to match proceeds from current sales to current inventory replacement costs. Also, because FIFO valuation increases profits, it results in higher income taxes.

Because of these flaws, accountants developed the second valuation method: *LIFO*, or last-in, first-out inventory valuation. LIFO is generally preferred today. LIFO assigns to goods going out of inventory the most recent—generally, a higher—

applicable cost: $4 in the Mammoth Widget case. The effect
of LIFO valuation, in periods of inflation, is to match more
closely current income and current costs. LIFO leaves in
inventory the older, lower costs. By reducing overall inventory valuation, then, LIFO reduces profits and reduces income taxes. Businesses can use the tax savings to buy new
materials or merchandise to replace the current higher-
valued merchandise.

The third method is average pricing. Averaging changes the
costs of units in inventory with each new purchase. For
example, let's say that in addition to its old $3 and $4 widgets,
Mammoth now produces 20 additional widgets at a cost of $5
each, for a total inventory of 50 widgets with a total cost of
$210 ($30 plus $80 plus $100). The company may decide to
value each widget sold at $4.20, a "weighted average"
amount. There are other methods of averaging, too. Averaging
dampens the effects of price changes.

To summarize FIFO, LIFO, and averaging, let's look at
Mammoth Widget once again. Inventory at the beginning of
the year is:

10 widgets @ $3 each	$30
20 widgets @ $4 each	80

During the year, Mammoth produces 20 more widgets at $5
each, so total inventory for the year, before sales, is:

10 widgets @ $3 each	$ 30
20 widgets @ $4 each	80
20 widgets @ $5 each	100
	$210

Now let's say that Mammoth sells 25 widgets during the year.
The end-of-year inventory valuations will be:

Under FIFO

5 widgets remaining @ $4 each	$ 20
20 widgets remaining @ $5 each	100
Inventory at end of year	$120
Charged to cost of sales	$ 90

Under LIFO

10 widgets remaining @ $3 each	$ 30
15 widgets remaining @ $4 each	60
Inventory at end of year	$ 90
Charged to cost of sales	$120

Under averaging

25 widgets remaining @ $4.20 each	$105
Inventory at end of year	$105
Charged to cost of sales	$105

There are, of course, numerous factors that enter into the computation of unit costs. In a manufacturing company, valuation of finished goods takes into consideration the initial costs of work in process, direct material costs and direct labor costs needed to finish the goods, plus a fair share of factory overhead. If a manufacturer uses standard costs for material charges to production, the firms will use a *variance account* to record differences between actual and standard costs. This variance account is closed into the factory overhead account at the end of the year. A similar treatment is used for standard labor costs.

Work in Process

Year-end valuation of work-in-process inventory, or partly completed goods, calculates not only the costs of materials and supplies but how far along the product is toward completion. A company computes values of raw materials at historical cost—whether by FIFO, LIFO, or an averaging method—or at standard costs, as mentioned above. Then, depending on steps taken toward completion, the company adds wage costs at either historical or standard rates plus the value of appropriate overhead.

For example, suppose the process of producing 1 unit of part A-102 requires 100 units of Alpha, then 20 hours of labor, then 25 units of Beta, then 3 hours of cleanup. Alpha costs $3 per unit, and labor is $12 per hour. Just 10 hours of labor have been expended so far. This tells us how far along part A-102 is in production. The maker of A-102 arrives at its work-in-process valuation this way:

100 units of Alpha @ $3/unit	$300
10 hours of labor @ $12/hour	120
Cost of work in process	$420, plus appropriate factory overhead

CONTROL OF INVENTORIES

Dollar valuations of inventories are important, but dollar valuations depend on the quantity and quality of inventories. And quantity and quality, in turn, depend on careful purchasing and effective security.

Purchasing Inventories

The guiding principle behind all purchasing is to obtain the quality needed at the lowest possible cost.

And quality matters. To choose one real-life example, a California manufacturer of troop carriers purchased low-priced bolts overseas. The specifications were identical to those of higher-priced bolts made in the United States. The manufacturer used the bolts without testing whether they met their specs. But when the personnel carriers were placed into service, the bolts failed; the carriers were useless as built. Well-thought-out purchasing procedures help guard against this kind of waste.

Efficient purchasing also aims to minimize cost. The components of the cost of a unit of material are (1) unit item cost; (2) unit purchasing (ordering) cost; and (3) unit holding (storage) cost.

The unit item cost is the price the supplier charges per unit. The unit purchasing cost is an internally generated figure. It is a per-unit calculation of all purchasing costs: salaries and

Table 4.1 Purchasing (Ordering) Cost Per Units Purchased

Units purchased (1)	Purchasing cost/unit (2) = $75/(1)
100	$0.7500
200	0.3750
300	0.2500
400	0.1875
500	0.1500
600	0.1250
700	0.1071
800	0.0938
900	0.0833
1,000	0.0750

expenses of the purchasing and receiving departments and incoming goods inspection department, internal transportation department costs for moving goods from receiving dock to storerooms, and related overhead items. For example, if a company processes 10,000 purchase orders a year at a total annual purchasing cost of $750,000, each purchase order costs $75. In general, the more units purchased per purchase order, the lower the purchasing cost per unit, as shown in table 4.1.

When goods come in, they must be stored. This holding or storage cost includes the rental, or rent equivalent, of the space in the storeroom or warehouse; insurance on the inventory; security for the goods; storeroom accounting costs; spoilage and breakage; and related overhead items. For example, if this total is $40,000 and the average of all inventory for the year is $800,000, the holding cost expressed as a percentage will be $40,000 divided by $800,000, or 5 percent.

Applying this 5 percent per unit holding cost, table 4.2 shows how storage costs rise for different quantities of inventory, assuming a unit item cost of $20. Notice that the more units ordered at one time, the higher the per-unit storage cost.

Table 4.2 Storage (Holding) Costs Per Unit Purchased

Units Purchased (1)	Average inventory (Units) (2) = (1)/2	Average inventory ($) (3) = (2) x $20	Total holding costs ($) (4) = (3) x 5%	Holding cost per unit ($) (5) = (4)/2,000
100	50	$ 1,000	$ 50	$0.0250
200	100	2,000	100	0.0500
300	150	3,000	150	0.0750
400	200	4,000	200	0.1000
500	250	5,000	250	0.1250
600	300	6,000	300	0.1500
700	350	7,000	350	0.1750
800	400	8,000	400	0.2000
900	450	9,000	450	0.2250
1,000	500	10,000	500	0.2500

Column (5) shows the cost per individual unit used during the year (2,000).

Every company would like to carry no inventory but have an instantaneous supply of material in the quantity and quality needed at the time of use—an impossible ideal. The opposite extreme is to buy a year's supply of material at the beginning of each year. This extreme is possible but highly inefficient; it would require a large storage area that would be used less and less as the year progressed.

Economic Order Quantity (EOQ)

One way to reconcile these two extremes is through the use of the *economic order quantity*, or *EOQ*, concept. The EOQ is the most efficient quantity to order at one time, given all the particular circumstances of a particular business. A business can chart the total unit cost of inventory by calculating per-unit purchasing and storage costs, then adding them together to develop a total per-unit cost curve. Figure 4.1

**Per-unit
storage cost in
dollars**

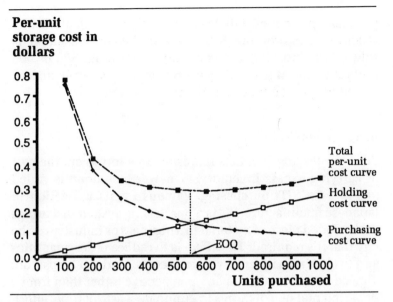

Figure 4.1 Economic Order Quantity

(based on tables 4.1 and 4.2) shows this curve. As the figure indicates, the EOQ is the lowest point on the total per-unit cost curve.

Several formulas have been developed to generate EOQ. One such formula is:

$$EOQ = \sqrt{\frac{2 \times (\text{purchase cost/order}) \times \text{usage (units/year)}}{(\text{invoice cost/unit}) \times (\text{holding cost in percent per year})}}$$

To see how this formula works, assume 2000 units used per year, each with a unit item cost of $20. Using the $75 unit purchasing and 5 percent holding costs mentioned above, we get this computation of EOQ:

$$EOQ = \sqrt{\frac{2 \times \$75 \times 2000}{\$20 \times 5\%}} = 547 \text{ units (approx.)}$$

That is, the most economical and efficient order quantity in these particular circumstances is 547 units. Purchasing department personnel will take the EOQ for each item into account when ordering. If the item in the above example is sold by the hundred, the company might order 500 or 600 units at a time; if it's sold by the dozen, then 45 or 46 dozens would be an economic order quantity.

Just-in-Time (JIT)

EOQ purchasing formulas represent an effort to cut the cost of carrying excess inventory. A newer technique is called *just-in-time (JIT)* purchasing. Famous for its utilization in Japanese manufacture, JIT is a purchasing system that brings each needed piece of material to a business or industry on the day that it's required. The effect is to reduce order quantities and to eliminate inventory storage costs. Under JIT, costs are viewed from a total company perspective rather than from a departmental one. JIT aims to eliminate waste of time, effort, and materials while improving productivity and quality.

The JIT purchasing concept works best in fast-flowing lines of production with few variations. As the number of variants increases the effectiveness of JIT diminishes. Management literature on JIT is mathematically oriented and emphasizes product flow, activities, costs, and simplification. JIT is an area worthy of further study. In complex manufacturing situations, making JIT work can be difficult. Those organizations that can implement JIT purchasing can realize many benefits, however. And some researchers find that the commonsense, teamwork-oriented philosophy behind JIT is beneficial even in complex manufacturing companies.

Security of Inventories

Loss and damage of inventories can reduce a company's profits. Security measures are not without expense, but the cost of security must be weighed against the savings a company can realize.

On a very minor level, many companies tolerate employee misuse of company supplies such as stationery, pens, staplers, and so on. Steps to prevent this pilferage, while they would have some costs, could save companies many hundreds of millions of dollars a year in the United States as a whole.

Businesses must protect inventories of finished goods ready for sale and of raw materials and supplies—some of which are themselves finished products, such as batteries or tires for an automobile manufacturer. Grading systems exist that require more security for some types of items than for others. The cost of an item as well as its character will determine its rank on the grading system. High-security inventory items include, for example:

1. Items of a high value-to-bulk ratio;
2. Items essential to a production process;
3. Items of great personal or resale utility; and
4. Fad items.

Several of these high-security inventory categories also present special problems relating to inventory control and purchasing.

Items of a high value-to-bulk ratio are, for example, gold, precious gems, expensive watches, collector coins, rare stamps, and the like. These types of items, being small, can be easily hidden, and their high value adds further incentive for pilferage or theft. Take the case of a jewelry store. The salesperson presents to a customer a tray of rings. The tray has slots; the salesperson should see that every slot is initially filled. When the tray is returned, the clerk has only to check that all the slots are filled or that the customer has a ring for each empty slot. Here, the physical layout of the display is used to control the inventory. The sales staff must also be educated in the proper handling of the merchandise and trained to watch for merchandise switching (substituting a fake ring in a slot, for example). A visible camera trained on the service area is also a deterrent against this kind of loss.

Items essential to the production process—such as chassis for cars or specialized lumber in a furniture company—are more an inventory control problem than a security problem, although some of these items may also be of high personal or resale value. Obviously, not having an automobile chassis to put on the production line will stop the productive process. Manufacturers must take great care to time purchase orders properly, to check the location of items in transit continually, and to anticipate problems caused by weather or suppliers' labor conditions. These cautions will help a company avoid shortages of vital materials.

Items of great personal or resale utility are those that can be readily used or sold by a thief: tires, batteries, computers, radios, TVs, VCRs, microwave ovens, sporting goods, and so on. These kinds of inventory require careful control. Often, control need not be high-tech, but it must exist and be implemented. For example, consider Sue's Service Station, which sells such items as tires and batteries. When Sue closes the cash register for the day, she takes the locked register tapes, the cash over the change fund, and the charge slips. The register is then ready for the night shift. Sue also counts expensive items with high personal or resale utility such as tires and batteries. When she arrives the next day, she counts these items again and compares the count to that of the day before. For every tire or battery missing, she should find a sales slip. The employees know that Sue can pinpoint any losses and that she will look to the employees to account for discrepancies.

Other items of this resale or personal use type must be counted correctly when received from suppliers. Items can disappear from the receiving department. If one department does both receiving and shipping, an employee can affix an address label to a newly arrived carton and a cooperating driver can take the item with the next outgoing load. The proceeds from such cooperative theft can be divided.

Also, empty containers can be sitting in the plant while the merchandise is disappearing out the shipping room door. The illicit traffic in radios, VCRs, and other such items is enormous. Constant vigilance by the security force and management is necessary to prevent this type of loss; thieves are ever open to new ideas and will take advantage of company equipment as well as of insufficiently alert company personnel.

Fad items like popular videotapes, this year's hot board game, or women's fashion items make up another class of items that must be controlled carefully. When the fad passes, the goods rapidly lose their value. Purchase and sales must be coordinated for control. Women's fashions departments of department stores often use a system of notifying the buyers when each item is sold. The buyer then uses his or her knowledge and best judgment in deciding whether to reorder. The reorder must be immediate to prevent loss of sales due to lack of merchandise. At the same time, the reorder must not be excessive, or there will be an oversupply when demand slackens. In the hula hoop mania of the 1950s, some manufacturers let production get ahead of sales, and when the mania stopped, they were left with huge unsold inventories. The story of oversupply was similar at the end of the Cabbage Patch Kids craze.

Security technologies available today are familiar to most of us as consumers. There are devices attached to merchandise that set off alarms at the exits if they are not removed. Magnetizing strips inserted in books in stores or libraries will also set off alarms unless deactivated. Large convex mirrors or closed-circuit TVs allow store managers to observe activity in the aisles. Surveillance cameras monitor public areas of banks and other financial institutions as well as jewelry stores and other retailers. (Note that a company must take care not to invade customers' privacy, opening the way to lawsuits.)

In many hotel and motel rooms, the TV is bolted down and security devices may be set off if the set is removed; pictures and other decorations may be screwed into the walls. There are physical barriers, too. A supermarket may install steel fencing with openings big enough for people to walk through but too small for shopping carts; this helps prevent the loss of shopping carts, a loss that can be expensive indeed. Some supermarkets use a "fifth wheel" that becomes operative when the cart goes over a curb, causing the cart to travel only in circles. Other companies use guards to examine packages leaving the premises. All in all, a large industry has grown up to fill the needs of businesses that face theft problems and want to overcome them.

EXAMPLES

Different Methods of Inventory Valuation

You are an accountant for Colossal Widget Manufacturing Company. Colossal gives you its inventory values for inventory at the end of the year 19X3 and inventory purchased during 19X4 (example 4.1). Colossal reports to you that they have sold 75 widgets during 19X4. What year-end valuations would you place upon Colossal's inventory, using FIFO and LIFO valuation methods?

Example 4.2 shows the solution. In general, LIFO valuation will produce lower inventory values because of the tendency of costs to rise, otherwise known as inflation. However, if the cost of inventory items is falling, FIFO will produce this effect.

Income Tax Effects of Inventory Valuation

Now let's take an example that demonstrates the impact of FIFO and LIFO valuations on a company's income and in-

Example 4.1

Widget Inventory as of December 31, 19X3

Units	Cost per unit	Total cost
20	$2.50	$ 50.00
25	3.00	75.00
35	4.00	140.00
40	4.50	180.00
Total value		$445.00

Purchases for the Year Ending December 31, 19X4

Units	Cost per unit	Total cost
10	$4.50	$ 45.00
30	5.00	150.00
Total cost		$195.00

---

come taxes for the year. Example 4.3 gives an extremely simplified computation of cost of goods sold and a condensed income statement. Compute the income tax and net income under FIFO inventory valuation and under LIFO inventory valuation, assuming tax at 40 percent.

Your solution should look like this:

	FIFO inventory	LIFO inventory
Sales	$700	$700
Less cost of goods sold	355	455
Less other expenses	45	45
Gross income	300	200
Income taxes @ 40%	120	80
Net income	$180	$120

Notice the differences between taxes and income under the two methods. LIFO has inventory lower and cost of goods sold higher, resulting in lower profits, and the income tax savings may be used to purchase further inventories at current prices. It may seem appealing to alternate between in-

Example 4.2

Widget Inventory for 19X4

Units	Cost per unit	Total cost
20	$2.50	$ 50.00
25	3.00	75.00
35	4.00	140.00
50	4.50	225.00
30	5.00	150.00
Total value		$640.00

FIFO Inventory Valuation

Units	Cost per unit	Total cost
0	$2.50	$ 0.00
0	3.00	0.00
0	4.00	0.00
30	4.50	135.00
30	5.00	150.00
Year-end inventory value		285.00
Charged to cost of sales		$355.00

LIFO Inventory Valuation

Units	Cost per unit	Total cost
20	$2.50	$ 50.00
25	3.00	75.00
15	4.00	60.00
0	4.50	0.00
0	5.00	0.00
Year-end inventory value		185.00
Charged to cost of sales		$455.00

---

ventory valuation methods to reduce tax liabilities. However, the IRS makes this method of tax reduction expensive by requiring prior years' inventories to be revalued under the new proposed method and the increased taxes for those years to be paid at the time of the changeover.

Example 4.3

Cost of goods sold (year ending December 31, 19X4)	FIFO	LIFO
Inventory at beginning of year	$300	$300
Plus purchases during year	340	340
Less inventory at end of year	285	185
Cost of goods sold	$355	$455

Income Statement
For Year Ending December 31, 19X4

	FIFO	LIFO
Sales	$700	$700
Less cost of goods sold	355	455
Less other expenses	345	245
Gross income	——	
Less income taxes @ 40%	——	
Net income	——	

SUMMARY

Inventories are assets that a business has acquired for sale or for use in the manufacture of goods for sale. In both merchandising and manufacturing businesses, the ideal is to minimize the dollar volume of inventory and yet allow sales and manufacturing to progress smoothly.

In merchandising, inventories are finished goods available for sale. Inventory information is used to ensure adequate supplies of inventory while minimizing overstocks. In manufacturing, inventories include finished goods, raw materials, and work in process.

Valuation in retail businesses depends on detailed records of original costs, markups, and market prices. Year-end inventory is valued at cost or market, whichever is lower.

Valuation in nonretail situations assigns costs to items gone from inventory in order to arrive at a value for inventory remaining at the end of the year. FIFO, LIFO, and averaging are the three approaches used. Work in process valuation also calculates how far a product has progressed toward completion.

Efficient purchasing is key to the control of both quantity and quality of inventories. EOQ and JIT are two methods used to promote efficient purchasing. Security measures to help protect inventories against loss or theft are important in many kinds of businesses.

5

Long-lived Assets

Long-lived assets are another category of assets that appear on most balance sheets. They usually make up a large part of a company's total assets.

Decisions about acquisition and management of long-lived assets are part of virtually every business, and these decisions can set the stage for future success—or failure. Because inflation is a fact of life in the present-day business world, a company that invests in a quality long-lived asset will gain a distinct competitive advantage in years to come. Income tax rules on depreciation of long-lived assets, as explained below, will allow the company to pay lower taxes now, and these cash savings will be worth more now than in the future. Also, competing firms entering the field in future years will generally have to pay higher initial prices and higher financing costs for the same type of asset. Thus the company that invests today can expect to enjoy a cash flow bonus later on. And this advantage becomes even greater once the asset is fully paid for. In many cases, for example, a company's ownership of a fully paid-for plant has made the difference between victory and defeat in a competitive business environment.

WHAT ARE LONG-LIVED ASSETS?

Long-lived assets include all assets with productive lives of more than one year. Often called *fixed assets*, long-lived assets consist of land, buildings, and equipment. Indeed, some companies' balance sheets refer to this category of assets as "Property, Plant, and Equipment."

The cost of a long-lived asset must be spread over the physical or economic life of the asset via depreciation. The income tax laws allow various methods of calculating the depreciation of an asset. A well-managed company will choose for each asset the most advantageous depreciation formula currently allowed, given the particular asset and the particular income tax regulations prevailing at the time.

TYPES AND VALUES OF LONG-LIVED ASSETS

For balance sheet purposes, the book value of a long-lived asset is its historical cost minus the amount of depreciation that has been charged to operations. Historical cost in this context means the original purchase price plus any and all other expenses the company has incurred in connection with acquiring the asset and readying it for productive use. In the case of buildings and equipment, the value determined by historical cost serves as the base for figuring depreciation on the asset.

Let's look at some specifics of how businesses establish costs in the three types of long-lived assets: land, buildings, and equipment.

Land

In this book, the term *land* refers to a place on which to put a business facility, such as an office building, plant, apartment house, or shopping center. (Agricultural land is a separate category and is not the subject here.)

Sometimes a business purchases land with nothing on it. The purchase price is developed from the escrow statement, excepting prepaid taxes, interest, and insurance. It is fairly easy to determine the price of the acreage, which generally includes the contract price, title search, title insurance, recording and notary fees, and legal fees—although in some cases, legal fees are charged to expense.

If the business purchases land with something on it that the buyer does not want, the expenses necessary to make the site usable are added to the above costs. These expenses consist of demolition costs less salvage value, if any.

If a business buys land with a facility that the buyer intends to keep, the contract price plus title search, title insurance, recording and notary fees, and perhaps legal fees are *prorated* between land and facility (building, parking lot, or whatever). The local assessor's figures or an appraisal of the property determines the prorated shares (i.e., proportionate parts) of the cost allocated to each part of the purchased real estate.

The most important point to keep in mind is that land is not depreciated. Land is not used up; it always remains a site—barring natural events such as earthquakes or tidal waves. Therefore, the company's operations are not charged with any part of the cost of the land. In cases of natural diminution or accretion of land, no change is made to the cost records unless the economic value of the site has decreased. And normally, there is no change in historical cost if the land becomes more valuable. As a result, in a time of fast-rising land values (the 1980s, for example), the cost of land as carried on a company's books will be much lower than its current market value.

Buildings

A facility built on land will last more than one year, but unlike land, it will undergo gradual deterioration and eventually will have to be renewed or replaced. Therefore, its cost must be charged on some basis to current and future operations—that is, depreciated. The basis for depreciation will be the cost of the building.

As mentioned, when a company buys land and building(s) as a single purchase, it prorates the historical cost between the land and the facility. If the company is going to use the facility in the condition in which it is purchased, that prorated cost is the asset cost of the facility. The prorated purchase prices of most residential and commercial rental properties, for example, are considered as asset costs. The new landlord does not disturb the tenants and does nothing to the building.

However, if the company is going to renovate a building or change its character—such as from apartments to offices—the costs of designing, drawing plans, demolition (less salvage), securing permits, securing bids, and mortgage payments during the planning stages are added to the prorated cost of the building. The actual cost of construction is also added, as are the mortgage payments during construction. ("Lost income" is not added, although many buyers wish it could be.)

Federal income tax regulations allow a short period of time for a new owner to make changes in an existing building and capitalize them. Cost accumulation stops when the contractor is finished and the owner inspects the project and accepts the keys. If the contractor still has uncompleted work, however, some monies can be reserved—put in escrow—up to a set date to ensure that the contractor will finish the job. In this situation, cost accumulation ends as of the close of escrow.

If a company is building a new facility from scratch, the facility's historical cost will include demolition of any existing structures (less salvage), site preparation, and the costs of designing, permits, construction, and so on, as well as mortgage payments through to the completion of construction. In some long-term projects, such as a major office tower, the lower floors may be rented before the whole structure is completed. In this kind of case, some part of the expenditures and some depreciation are charged against the rental receipts.

Equipment

Land and buildings constitute *realty* (real estate), which is defined as land and those things permanently attached to the land. All other—that is, not permanently attached—tangible possessions are called *personalty*. There are some subtleties to the distinction between realty and personalty, however. If an apartment tenant, with the landlord's permission, attaches a ceiling light fixture over the dining table, the lamp is the tenant's personalty. The tenant must restore the property to its original lampless condition when he or she vacates. But if the tenant installs the lamp without the landlord's permission, the lamp may immediately become the landlord's realty, because it is attached to the building.

In business, by contrast, even attached equipment remains the personalty of the business. For example, if a butcher bolts a refrigerated display case to the floor, the display case is the personalty of the butcher, because it is a trade fixture and was never meant to be part of the realty.

Once equipment is defined, its cost is the accumulation of all the costs necessary to install it and prepare it for use. If an eastern factory purchases a lathe from a midwestern manufacturer, the costs of freight, any insurance paid during transportation, and the setting up, leveling, and testing of the lathe are all considered part of the historical cost.

If equipment is designed and manufactured in-house, its cost is the accumulation of design, construction, assembly, and testing costs, plus a prorated share of the various over-heads that relate to all these processes.

In a company's books there may be many equipment ac-counts, each covering a single class of equipment, although for purposes of simplification the balance sheet usually lumps all equipment under one heading. The classes of equipment might include factory machinery; trucks; autos; internal transportation (overhead conveyors, escalators, fork-lift trucks, etc.); computers; and other such classifications. One reason for these separate accounting classifications can be for control purposes, such as continued maintenance on trucks, licensing requirements, and the like. Classifications are also useful, however, for accounting purposes. Different groups of assets have differing useful lives. Ultimately, then, accounting by equipment classification applies suitable de-preciation expense to the appropriate areas of the business.

METHODS OF DEPRECIATION

Depreciation is the accounting convention used to spread the cost of a building or piece of equipment over either the physical life or the economic life of the asset.

When a business buys an asset and places it in service, it may pay cash or pay under some form of payment schedule. There is no necessary relationship between the payment term and the depreciation period. The business uses as its period for depreciation the physical or the economic life as the asset is designed and used, whichever is shorter. In some cases, the physical life of the asset can be longer than the economic life; an oil platform is an example. Depreciation, as we'll see, has numerous income tax implications and numerous effects on financial statements.

Once a company has decided whether to use the physical or the economic life of a piece of realty or personalty as its period of depreciation, it decides on a method of allocating the cost over that life. The mathematical formulas for depreciation are rather simple. All utilize the asset's historical cost and length of useful life. Some of these formulas also take into account the asset's salvage value—the expected value of the asset at the end of its life. In periods of price instability, salvage value can be difficult to determine, however; and it becomes increasingly difficult over a long term.

Let's look at four general depreciation methods. The first is the "straight-line" method. Then there are the "accelerated" methods: sum of the years' digits and declining balance. Finally, there are per-hour or per-unit methods.

Straight-line Depreciation

Straight-line depreciation is the simplest of all methods to use and compute. Straight-line depreciation assumes the asset to lose the same proportion of its total value each year of its service life and allocates the same amount of asset cost (depreciation expense) to operations each year. The formula for straight-line depreciation, in other words, is simply cost (less salvage value) divided by number of terms (such as years or months) of life.

Let's take as an example an asset costing $85,000, with an estimated salvage value of $5,000. Its life is estimated to be 12 years. (Calculations will be rounded to the nearest dollar.) In straight-line depreciation, the formula for cost allocation is:

$$\text{Depreciation expense per term} = \frac{\text{Asset} - \text{Estimated salvage value}}{\text{Number of terms}}$$

If the terms for the $85,000 asset were months, the formula would be:

Depreciation expense per month

$$= \frac{\$85,000 - \$5,000}{144 \text{ months}} = \frac{\$80,000}{144} = \$556 \text{ per month}$$

Note that a company must make some rule about how to treat the first and last years of service of a long-lived asset. This rule can be simple. One approach, for example: In the year an asset is placed in service, the depreciation expense is treated as if the asset was used that whole year; then no depreciation expense is taken in the year the asset is disposed of. Another approach is the half-year-rule: If an asset is placed in service during the first half of a year, the depreciation expense is treated as if the asset was used during the whole year; if it's placed in service in the second half, a half-year's depreciation expense is assumed. Or the terms can be quarter-years or even months. In the case of months, the year is divided into 12 equal parts for accounting purposes.

Organizations spend a great deal of time studying the tax code so as to be able to choose the method of depreciation most beneficial to them in terms of the "time value of money." (Money received today is more valuable than money received tomorrow, because of inflation. In tax terms, taxes saved today are more valuable than taxes saved tomorrow.) But the IRS has always accepted straight-line depreciation, because straight-line was the major method used when the income tax was created.

Other depreciation methods, by contrast, accelerate cost recovery. That is, they put more depreciation expense in the earlier years. Since depreciation is an expense deducted from a business's income, *accelerated depreciation* reduces income taxes in the earlier years, leaving the company with more cash. However, the income taxes are only deferred; tax liability will rise later in the life of the asset, as depreciation expense gets smaller.

Sum-of-the-Years' Digits Depreciation

One type of accelerated depreciation is *sum of the years' digits*, a method created before the 1986 Tax Reform Act. The first step is to generate a number that is the sum of the digits from 1 to the number of terms of life of the asset. For the $85,000, 12-year example we're using, let's take a year as the depreciation term this time. The sum, then, is $1 + 2 + 3 + 4 + 5 + 6 + 7 + 8 + 9 + 10 + 11 + 12 = 78$. The number 78 becomes the denominator of a reducing fraction. For a given year, the numerator of the fraction is the term in reverse: 12 in year 1, 11 in year 2, and so on. The asset cost minus salvage is multiplied by this fraction:

$$\text{Depreciation expense in year 1} = \frac{12}{78} \times \$80,000 = \$12,308$$

Table 5.1 shows how sum-of-the-years' digits depreciation will affect the charge to operations and the book value of this asset over its 12 years of life.

Table 5.1 Sum-of-the-Years' Digits Depreciation Schedule—$85,000 Asset Cost, $5,000 Estimated Salvage Value, and 12-Year Life

	Book value end of year (1)	Accumulated depreciation (2)	Depreciation expense (3) = ($85,000 – $5,000) x		
Cost	$85,000				
Year 1	72,692	$12,308	12/78	=	$12,308
2	61,410	23,590	11/78	=	11,282
3	51,154	33,846	10/78	=	10,256
4	41,923	43,077	9/78	=	9,231
5	33,718	51,282	8/78	=	8,205
6	26,539	58,461	7/78	=	7,179
7	20,385	64,615	6/78	=	6,154
8	15,257	69,743	5/78	=	5,128
9	11,154	73,846	4/78	=	4,103
10	8,077	76,923	3/78	=	3,077
11	6,026	78,974	2/78	=	2,051
12	5,000	80,000	1/78	=	1,026

Declining-Balance Depreciation

A second accelerated depreciation method is *declining-balance depreciation*. This method, too, accelerates cost recovery into the earlier years. The formula for declining-balance depreciation uses no salvage value, because a value remains under this system. The declining-balance approach is especially advantageous for tax purposes. Income tax laws classify assets as 125 percent, 150 percent, or 200 percent assets. The general formula for declining-balance depreciation is:

$$\text{Depreciation in term } t = \text{Depreciation \% (125, 150, or 200)} \times \frac{\text{Book value in term } t - 1}{\text{Total depreciable life}}$$

If our sample asset is classified a 150 percent declining-balance asset, the formula for term 1 (the first year) will be:

$$\text{Depreciation in term } 1 = 1.5 \times \frac{\$85,000}{12} = \$10,625$$

After the first year, the formula is applied to the end-of-year book value of the preceding year each time. Table 5.2a shows how this works.

Note, however, that in table 5.2a the ending book value of $17,120 is greater than the asset's estimated $5,000 salvage value. To decrease the book value to the salvage estimate, a rule exists that changes the end of the period into a straight-line calculation. Application of this rule reduces the $25,556 book value at the end of year 9 to $5,000 in equal increments of $6,852 per year over 3 years. That is, years 10 to 12 in table 5.2a become those shown in table 5.2b.

Per-Unit or Per-Hour Depreciation

Per-unit or *per-hour depreciation* applies generally to manufacturing equipment whose expected total units of output or

Table 5.2a Depreciation Schedule for 150% Declining Balance—
$85,000 Asset Cost and 12-Year Life

	Book value end of year (1)	Accumulated depreciation (2)	Depreciation expense (3)
Cost	$85,000		
Year 1	74,375	$10,625	$10,625
2	65,078	19,922	9,297
3	56,943	28,057	8,135
4	49,825	35,175	7,118
5	43,597	41,403	6,228
6	38,147	46,853	5,450
7	33,379	51,621	4,768
8	29,207	55,793	4,172
9	25,556	59,444	3,651
10	22,361	62,639	3,195
11	19,566	65,434	2,795
12	17,120	67,880	2,446

Table 5.2b Alternative Depreciation Schedule for 150% Declining
Balance—$85,000 Asset Cost and 12-Year Life—to Reduce Book
Value to Estimated Salvage Value of $5,000

	Book value end of year (1)	Accumulated depreciation (2)	Depreciation expense (3)
Year 9	$25,556	$59,444	$3,651
10	18,704	66,296	6,852
11	11,852	73,148	6,852
12	5,000	80,000	6,852

whose total number of operating hours is known. Per-unit or
per-hour depreciation, by allowing depreciation to be taken
based on the usage that the equipment has undergone, results

in a reasonably accurate representation of the current value of the asset. This method gives a constant per-unit or per-hour cost, but depreciation expense varies from year to year depending on the rate of production.

Per-Unit Depreciation

The general formula for per-unit depreciation is:

$$\text{Depreciation expense per unit} = \frac{\text{Cost} - \text{Estimated salvage value}}{\text{Estimated units to be made}}$$

For example, if the $85,000 asset were a machine designed to produce a certain part and the estimated number of parts to be made were 100,000, then each part must bear $.80 of the asset's cost:

$$\text{Depreciation expense per part} = \frac{\$85,000 - \$5,000}{100,000} = \$.80$$

Table 5.3 represents a possible scenario under per-unit depreciation. Note that in year 9 in the table, 10,000 parts are produced, but that 95,000 units have already been used in computing depreciation expense in years 1 through 8. Only another 5,000 units need be used for depreciation expense to bring the book value down to $5,000. In year 9, therefore, 5,000 additional units are produced with no depreciation charged against them. And in years 10, 11, and 12 there are 24,000 units produced with no depreciation expense charged against them. In years 9 through 12, then, profits will be higher, if all other variables are comparable.

Per-Hour Depreciation

Per-hour depreciation uses reasoning similar to that of the per-unit method. The machine or tool is designed to operate for so many hours and the allocated depreciation expense is prorated to those hours:

$$\text{Depreciation expense per year} = \frac{\text{Cost} - \text{Estimated salvage value}}{\text{Estimated hours of use}}$$
$$\text{x Actual hours used in year}$$

Many machines are rated for hours of use. Assume that the machine in our example, if properly maintained, will produce good parts for 20,000 hours. Based on its $80,000 depreciable value, its usage cost will therefore be $4 per hour of usage. Each year the actual hours of usage are multiplied by $4 to determine the depreciation charge for the year.

Comparison of Depreciation Methods

The priorities of a business will affect its choice of depreciation method. The straight-line method is the easiest to apply, but as production varies and the depreciation charge remains

Table 5.3   Per-Unit Depreciation Schedule—$85,000 Asset Cost, $5,000 Estimated Salvage Value

	Number of parts produced	Depreciation expense
Year 1	5,000	$ 4,000
2	10,000	8,000
3	12,000	9,600
4	16,000	12,800
5	15,000	12,000
6	14,000	11,200
7	12,000	9,600
8	11,000	8,800
	95,000	76,000
9	5,000	4,000
	5,000	_____
10	9,000	_____
11	8,000	_____
12	7,000	
	129,000	$80,000

constant, the gross profit will vary. With the per-unit and per-hour methods, the depreciation varies with production and the profit percentage remains constant. In the accelerated methods—sum of the years' digits and declining balance—the depreciation charge is accelerated so as to reduce income taxes in the early years.

Congress is continually passing income tax legislation allowing new depreciation methods, and the Internal Revenue Service continually issues regulations and tables to support Congress's intent. Against this backdrop of constant change, businesses can legally depreciate assets under numerous different schedules, often gaining tax advantages thereby.

To be sure, once a company depreciates an asset by one method for income tax purposes, it cannot change the method for that asset. But if the company buys another asset of the same type, it can use another acceptable method for the new asset.

To give you a sense of the options available at this time, under the Tax Reform Act of 1986 the allowable depreciation rules include the following eight accelerated cost recovery systems (ACRS) classes:

- Three-year, 5-year, 7-year, and 10-year classes using 200 percent declining balance ("double-declining balance") with a switch-over to straight-line depreciation.
- Fifteen-year and 20-year classes using 150 percent declining balance with a switch-over to straight-line.
- Residential rental real estate in a 27.5-year class using straight-line.
- Nonresidential rental real estate in a 31.5-year class using straight-line.

Generally, ACRS rules apply to all eligible tangible and intangible property put in service after December 31, 1986. Certain property, however, is not eligible for ACRS treatment and must be depreciated under an alternative system. Under the new tax rules, it is possible for a business to contend with three sets of depreciation rules. In view of this complexity, many firms leave decisions about depreciation to their accountants or financial managers. For the reader who wants to pursue the subject further, the latest edition of IRS publication 534 on depreciation gives the latest tax wrinkles.

LEASING VERSUS BUYING

Should a company lease or buy a long-lived asset? Financially speaking, this decision hinges on a careful analysis of the respective costs and benefits of leasing versus buying.

In order to lease, a company generally has to show financial responsibility (proper credit rating) and put down a deposit. Then payments, which may include maintenance, begin. The company knows what the monthly cost of the use of the asset will be: regular payments plus the interest loss for a month on the deposit. The company must decide whether the package presented by the lessor makes economic sense. Arguments of economic sense can also be made for ownership of the asset. Often, however, a company finds itself weighing a would-be lessor's thoughtfully prepared program against its own less well prepared program. For this reason, a prospective lessee—or perhaps prospective owner—must study carefully each lease contract.

When a company leases an asset, it loses the depreciation and tax benefits of ownership but often incurs a lower monthly payment schedule (if it didn't, the company would probably buy). Under leasing, too, a company often is not responsible for maintenance costs; and it is usually easier to cancel a lease than to cancel ownership. Leasing is a type of off-balance-sheet financing. That is, lease liabilities are not required to appear on the balance sheet—although they often do appear in balance sheet footnotes—so a company may appear to have less liabilities than it actually has.

When a company buys a long-lived asset, by contrast, it is liable for costs of maintenance and repair, but it gains depreciation and tax benefits. Even more important is the benefit of asset ownership over the long term. In time, every lease must be renegotiated, and the new lease rates may make the business unprofitable. Or the owner of the asset may not want to renew the lease, leaving the business stranded.

Some tenants will go to any length to ensure their business space. For example, a realtor in San Francisco cannot buy the building in which he has his business because the landlord will not sell it. The realtor has been in this location for over 25 years, renegotiating the lease every 5 years and offering to extend the lease 5 more years with a modest increase in rent. The offer had always been accepted. The realtor maintains that the price paid over the years has been a bargain. However, when the landlord dies, the landlord's heirs, faced with a long-term lease at below-market rental, may well be inclined to accept the realtor's offer to purchase the property.

DISPOSAL OF LONG-LIVED ASSETS

Eventually there comes a time when the disposal of a long-lived asset is necessary. The asset may be worn out (machinery), obsolete (electronics), or no longer profitable or useful to the business.

Disposal of an asset by sale has some income tax implications. If the asset sells for more than its current book value (its depreciated value), the capital gain is taxable. The company computes the depreciation to the date of sale under its normal depreciation method, then measures the price received against the updated book value to determine gain. The company's income statement shows the gain as an extraordinary item. (How the gain is shown on the income tax return depends on the current tax regulations.) By the same token, if a company sells an asset for less than the book value, the loss reduces current income and thus the income taxes in the year of sale. Other methods of disposal (exchange, rent, etc.) each involve their own sets of income tax consequences and benefits. As a general rule, a company should consult a tax professional when considering any disposal of long-lived assets.

Trade-in is one option. For example, Sharpe Tools decides to trade in a five-year-old diestamping machine for a new one of like kind. The old machine has been depreciated to reflect its use up to the date of trade, and its book value is now $3,500. The cost of a new machine will be the book value of the old machine plus cash paid and/or liabilities assumed. After some negotiation, a machinery supplier agrees to sell Sharpe a new diestamper, allowing $3,900 for the trade-in and taking $10,800 in cash. Sharpe accepts the offer. The cost of the new diestamper to Sharpe, then, is the book value of the old machine, $3,500, plus the cash given in the purchase, $10,800, for a total of $14,300. This is called the "adjusted basis."

Land and buildings, because of changing markets, present special challenges and special opportunities. For example, a company may have a store or branch or plant in a poor location, where continued operation is going to reduce over-all profitability. What should the company do? In many cases, the company shuts down the facility and keeps the property on the books. This response, however, can produce an even greater loss. There are better solutions. One solution may be to rent the facility to another type of business that has a logical interest in the area. If a bank, for instance, finds that some neighborhoods no longer profitably support branch banks, it may consolidate a few branches and rent out the vacated spaces to retailers. Or an oil company may close stations and rent them to a restaurant chain. The company with excess facility may increase profits by becoming a landlord to new types of enterprises, because if the demand for the space is strong enough, the company may be able to secure a percentage lease; under this kind of lease the landlord shares in the tenant's sales as well as receiving rental payments.

Another solution to an unprofitable location may be to effect a tax-free exchange of unwanted property for property more suitable for the company's purposes. The company terminating its activity in the facility sells it to another company that can use it. The seller trades the net equity of the old facility into the new facility (or into new land on which to build a suitable facility). This reduces the basis of the new property and thus effectively defers any taxable gain. A lawyer competent in this type of transaction should structure the trade. As a condition of the sale, the buyer and the seller agree to cooperate in effecting the deal so that the title company follows detailed instructions ensuring a correctly executed tax-free exchange.

There is another side to the realty ownership coin. Disposal of property may present challenges, but in rising real estate markets, ownership of property can also be a major source of funds.

For example, a company can often mortgage realty to buy new commercial or residential buildings. Despite inflation and rising markets, the appreciation in value of physical facilities seldom gets much attention from management. Normally, company accountants do not revalue real property upward on the books, so any appreciation is unrecorded; the historical cost (less depreciation) remains. If a company looks to the actual current market value of its real property, however, mortgaging can have major potential benefits. In this situation, a company can reduce its taxes by:

- Adding to expenses the interest on the mortgage placed on the old building.
- Deducting from new rental income (1) rental operating expenses, (2) interest on the loans assumed on the

rental property, and (3) depreciation expense of the rental property. In the earlier years of ownership of the new property, this expense allocation can even create a loss for income tax purposes.

At the same time, the company benefits from the payoff on the loans, which after a set period of time (20, 25, 30, or however many years) leaves the original property unencumbered. Meanwhile, if the new property has been properly selected, it will appreciate in value.

In fact, a company that pursues an aggressive policy of trading or refinancing and purchase of new property may well find itself producing more income through its real estate holdings than through its regular operations. If a company invests money received from a mortgage in an area where prices are advancing at a rate higher than the inflation rate, it may be possible in a few years to refinance the new property and gain enough money to pay off the mortgage on the old property or use the money to buy new property—and so on and on. A company can often buy a facility at less than its worth, because its owner has failed to recognize the property's increased value. A word of warning, however: Tax regulations change constantly, and a competent tax professional should be consulted in every real estate transaction.

EXAMPLE

Income and Tax Consequences of Different Depreciation Methods

This example will investigate some implications of the various methods of depreciation. Three identical companies, Black Corporation, White Company, and Gray Brothers, each purchase a flux capacitor for $100,000. Each flux capacitor is estimated to have a useful life of 5 years and no salvage value.

Black Corporation uses straight-line depreciation, so it charges annual depreciation expense according to the formula:

$$\text{Depreciation per year} = \frac{\$100,000}{5} = \$20,000$$

White Company utilizes the sum of the years' digits. This sum is 15 (1 + 2 + 3 + 4 + 5). Thus depreciation in year 1 is 5/15 of $100,000, depreciation in year 2 is 4/15 of $100,000, and so forth.

Gray Brothers uses a 200 percent declining balance. Its depreciation formula, then, is:

$$\text{Depreciation in year t} = 200\% \times \frac{\text{Book value in year t} - 1}{5}$$

Given this information, prepare depreciation schedules for Black, White, and Gray. Which method will result in the lowest taxable income in year 1? In year 3? What impacts will the different methods have on the three companies' balance sheets?

Example 5.1 summarizes the annual depreciation under the three methods. All other things being equal, the company

Example 5.1

Methods of Depreciation Comparison

Initial cost: $100,000
Useful life: 5 years

Year	Black Corp. Straight line	White Co. Sum of years	Gray Bros. 200% declining
1	$20,000	$33,333	$40,000
2	20,000	26,667	24,000
3	20,000	20,000	14,400
4	20,000	13,333	8,640
5	20,000	6,667	5,184
Total	$100,000	$100,000	$92,224

---

that will pay the lowest taxes in year 1 will be the company with the highest depreciation expense, namely Gray Brothers, with its 200 percent declining balance. In year 3, however, straight-line and sum-of-the-years' digits methods will result in the same low taxes. Note that Gray Brothers has the highest depreciation in year 1 but the lowest in years 3 through 5. Gray enjoys improved cash flow early in the life of the asset but will pay more later on, since most of the flux capacitor's cost has been recovered in years 1 and 2 under Gray's method.

Also, because the three methods result in different book values, the three companies' long-lived assets will have different balance sheet values. The effect is to make these companies seem less comparable on paper. However, if you are comparing firms and you know their depreciation methods, you can make adjustments to compensate for these seeming differences.

SUMMARY

Long-lived assets, or assets with productive lives of more than one year, include land, buildings, and equipment. Depreciation is a method of allocating the cost of an asset over its physical or economic life. Land does not lose its place utility, so it is not depreciated. Buildings and equipment use up utility over time, so depreciation measures this loss of utility. The basis for depreciation—and for long-lived assets' values on a company's books—is the historical cost of the asset in each case. This cost includes the purchase price plus any and all costs required to prepare the asset for use.

The most commonly used methods of depreciation are straight-line, sum of the years' digits, declining balance, and per unit or per hour. Each method has an effect on a company's income tax liability, and companies may choose the method that will be most advantageous. The accelerated methods speed cost recovery in the early years, resulting in lower income taxes in those years.

The choice of leasing versus buying assets requires careful analysis of the costs and benefits of each alternative.

Disposal of long-lived assets presents both challenges and opportunities. Sale of an asset can have income tax consequences. But there are many ways to use realty to generate funds for the acquisition of other assets or for other purposes, given the long history of inflation.

Liabilities

6 Current Payables

Current payables are on the liabilities or "owed" side of the balance sheet. The central concept to keep in mind in connection with current payables is that every current payable represents an extension of credit to the company. As in every credit situation, a company's ability and willingness to meet its obligations are of foremost concern to its creditors. Every company must handle its current payables in such a way as to earn each creditor's confidence, so as to continue to receive credit in years to come.

Other entities interested in a company's current payables include business and financial analysts and banks and other lenders. As chapter 9 will explain, these outside analysts compare key ratios (proportionate relationships) among current payables, assets, and equity—along with other ratios—to help them evaluate a company as a prospect for an extension of credit, a loan, or a capital investment. So in a very practical sense, current payables can determine a company's future.

WHAT ARE CURRENT PAYABLES?

Current payables, or current liabilities, are amounts a business owes to outside entities that are payable within one year of the balance sheet date. Trade accounts payable are amounts owed by a business to its suppliers of goods and services, and this chapter focuses primarily on this class of payable. Other current payables include:

- Short-term interest-bearing debt;
- Any currently payable portion of the principal on long-term debt (see chapter 7);
- Current interest on both short- and long-term debts;
- Withholdings from employees' earnings;
- Company taxes due currently; and
- Accruals that will come due at some point in the year, such as vacation pay.

CONTROL MATTERS

The proper handling of trade accounts payable plays an important part in establishing a company's creditworthiness and overall financial soundness. As with accounts receivable (chapter 3), separation of functions helps pinpoint any problems and helps prevent loss, pilferage, or other mishandling of funds. Separation of functions also helps ensure that the company gets what it pays for.

Where payables are concerned, separation of functions means separation of purchasing, receiving, inspection, storage, and accounts payable responsibilities. Purchasing means placing orders for goods or materials; receiving means accepting delivery of the orders when they arrive; and the accounts payable department has the job of making payments. In a very small business, one person may be able to handle all these functions. But in larger companies, each phase should be done separately and carefully controlled and recorded. Imagine what would happen, for example, if all the employees of a large department store were involved in purchasing, receiving, and paying for goods. Unwise purchases, confusion, shortages and overages, and many opportunities for fraud and errors would result.

Let's see how control procedures work at one sample company. Figure 6.1 diagrams the sequence of events in simplified form, as numbered here.

Hoffman Plastics needs a new supply of corrugated cardboard shipping cartons.

1. A storeroom employee prepares a requisition in duplicate and has it countersigned by an authorizing person. One copy of the requisition goes to the purchasing department; the sender keeps a second copy for possible follow-up. The purchasing department reviews the requisition and, after obtaining competitive bids, selects Robinson Fibre & Pulp to supply the cartons.

2. Then purchasing prepares a purchase order. One or more copies of the order go to Robinson Fibre. Copies also go to Hoffman's storeroom department, to Hoffman's receiving department to alert them of the order, and to Hoffman's incoming inspection department. Purchasing retains still another copy for follow-up if needed. At this point, receiving personnel note that the cartons are expected and make sure that adequate space will be available to store them.

3. Robinson ships the goods with a packing slip.

4. When the cartons arrive, Hoffman's receiving personnel count the cartons and prepare a receiving report in duplicate. The original report goes to purchasing as notification that the order has been fulfilled. The receiving department

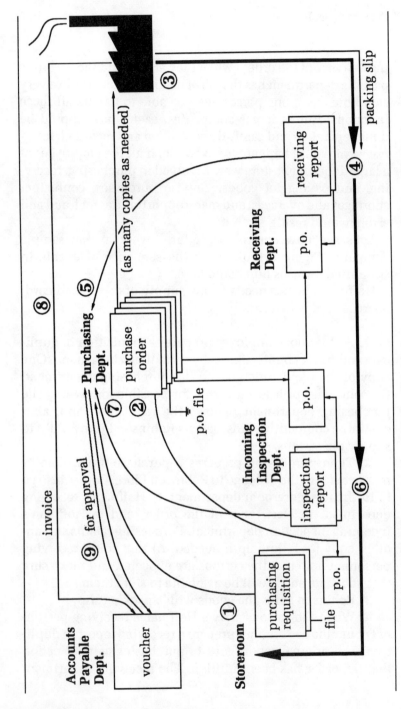

Figure 6.1 The Purchasing to Accounts Payable Routine

keeps the second copy along with its copy of the purchase order.

5. Purchasing checks the receiving report against the original purchase order to resolve any discrepancies.

6. The inspection department, notified of the cartons' arrival, inspects them and prepares an inspection report.

7. This report, too, goes to purchasing for review, while the inspection department retains a copy with its copy of the purchase order. Throughout all these phases, purchasing has maintained a file of purchase orders by number, attaching to each order all relevant documents received. In keeping with the principle of separation of functions, however, payment of the invoice for the cartons involves separate channels.

8. The invoice goes directly from Robinson Fibre to Hoffman's accounts payable department. Accounts payable prepares a voucher specifying Robinson's name, address, and other identification, together with terms of purchase, invoice price (gross or net, as discussed below), accounting distribution, and necessary approvals (see figure 2.1, page 29).

9. Accounts payable records the invoice in a register and sends the invoice with the voucher to purchasing for approval of payment.

10. When approved, the documents are returned to accounts payable. This approval, in effect, states that the cartons were ordered and were delivered in the proper quantity and quality, and that Hoffman now has a liability to pay. Any shortages, back orders, or other complications are noted so that only correct items are paid for.

When payment day arrives, Hoffman follows the kinds of check-writing precautions detailed in chapter 2. The check is prepared and sent to the authorized signer with the Robinson cartons payment voucher. Generally, a single signature is appropriate for checks up to some predetermined large amount. The check signer reviews the voucher and the signatures on it to ascertain that everyone has followed the prescribed control steps and that all stages have been properly approved.

This kind of system, with its line of approvals and separation of domains of responsibility, will go far to prevent mistakes or abuses in purchasing and cash disbursements.

DISCOUNTS AND TIMING OF PAYMENTS

Two kinds of discounts, or reductions in prices, are available to businesses: trade discounts and cash discounts. In the case of cash discounts, a company's payment procedure can have a substantial impact on its cash flow.

Trade Discounts

It is up to a company's purchasing department to monitor the *trade discounts* offered by all suppliers. Trade discounts vary from industry to industry. They are governed by trade practice—established custom in a given industry—and by an organization's position in that industry's merchandising chain. The closer a purchaser is to the source of an item, the greater the discount off the retail price will be.

For example, a certain size and type of vertical window blind may have a $100 retail price. Suppose the merchandising chain consists of the blind's manufacturer, a window-treatments wholesaler, and a department store. The manufacturer may offer trade discount terms of "40/20." This means that the department store gets a 40 percent discount, paying 60 percent of retail, or $60. The wholesaler gets a 20 percent discount off that $60, paying $48 ($60 minus $12). If there are more sellers in the chain, there will be more discounts. In order to simplify computations, companies usually express what they will pay as a single percentage of retail. In this example, the wholesaler would express its percentage as 48 percent. By the same token, if the discount terms were

40/20/10, the wholesaler's percentage would be 43.2 percent. This form of selling allows businesses at all positions on the merchandising chain to make use of the same catalogues and price lists. Each company computes its purchase cost by applying the appropriate percentage to the retail price.

Cash Discounts

Cash discounts, as you will recall, are discounts offered by vendors as incentives for prompt payment. For example, a "2/30" discount means that a 2 percent discount is allowed if an invoice is paid within 30 days of the invoice date. Available discounts should never be wasted. As chapter 3 explained, a discount can amount to the equivalent of a very good investment indeed.

A well-managed company will set up a system for making payments so as to use cash payment terms in the most advantageous way feasible—but so as to avoid paying any invoice needlessly early. Some companies issue checks according to a strict timetable: weekly, biweekly, or monthly, perhaps. But rigid schedules result in paying some invoices too late to receive cash discounts and paying some before they are due. Timing of disbursements can be an efficient means of controlling disbursement of funds. Accounts payable should categorize each invoice according to its due date. That is, an invoice from a local company dated June 10 with terms of 2/10, n/30 should be mailed June 20 for the discount. Accounts payable should check the files each day to ensure that each invoice is paid on its appointed date. This system accomplishes on-time payment to creditors while holding cash as long as possible.

A company's mode of accounting for current payables can assist in the disbursements control effort. There are two methods for recording invoices: gross and net.

The most common method, the gross method, is to record invoices at the gross (full) invoice price and to take the discount at the time the invoice is paid. The difference between the gross invoice price and the cash paid to the creditor is then credited to a "discounts earned" account and appears as extraordinary income on the company's income statement. But this method has a flaw. If a discount could have been taken but was not, no record is kept of the lost discount, and there is no way to see how many discounts have been lost.

A better method is the net method. This method requires that the invoice be recorded net of the discount. This method effectively functions as an internal control to ensure that all cash discounts offered are taken. If the payment is late, the company must pay the gross invoice amount and debit the difference between the gross and the discounted amount to a "discounts lost" account. The balance in this account will be zero if accounts payable takes advantage of all available discounts. If any cash discounts are not taken, however, entries will appear in the discounts lost account. Any balance in that account at year's end will appear as extraordinary expense on the income statement. This type of accounting is called "exception principle accounting" and allows management to know when unexpected events occur. Under this method, management can examine the reasons for failure to take discounts and take corrective action.

EXAMPLE

Discounts on Payables

Here is your chance to analyze a range of trade and cash discounts on current payables.

You are in charge of accounts payable at your company. You have a list (example 6.1) of invoices to be paid. Your company's policy is to take advantage of all available cash discounts, but also to pay on the last day allowed. All the

Example 6.1

List of Current Accounts Payable

Company	Invoice date	Terms	Invoice amount
ABC Repair Co.	25-May	2/10, n/30	$ 600
Sue's Office Supply	9-Jun	net 30	75
Ted's Manufacturing	15-Jun	4/10, 2/30, n/60	2,200
Spark Electric Co.	10-Jun	net 15	350
DynaSystems Inc.	15-Jun	1/5, n/30	1,700
Colonial Maintenance	29-May	2/10, n/30	250
Barron Realty	20-Jun	net 10	1,000
Premier Equipment Co.	3-Jun	3/15, n/60	4,500
			$10,675

invoices are from local companies. On what dates and for what amounts should the checks be issued?

Example 6.2 gives the answer. Note the savings in cash, not to mention the benefit of having the use of the cash up until the payment date in each case.

SUMMARY

Current payables represent extensions of credit to a company, and the relationships among current payables, assets, and equity are among yardsticks used to gauge a company's financial health. Current payables include all amounts payable within one year of the balance sheet date. Trade accounts payable are the major category; other categories include short-term debt, taxes, and so on.

Separation of functions among purchasing, receiving, inspection, storing, and accounts payable is key to proper management of current payables.

Example 6.2

List of Payment Dates and Amount Paid

Company	Invoice date	Payment date	Amount
ABC Repair Co.	25-May	4-Jun	$ 588
Sue's Office Supply	9-Jun	9-Jul	75
Ted's Manufacturing	15-Jun	25-Jun	2,112
Spark Electric Co.	10-Jun	25-Jun	350
DynaSystems Inc.	15-Jun	20-Jun	1,683
Colonial Maintenance	29-May	8-Jun	245
Barron Realty	20-Jun	30-Jun	1,000
Premier Equipment Co.	3-Jun	18-Jun	4,365
			$10,418

- -

	Original invoice	$10,675
	Paid	10,418
	Savings	$ 257

Trade discounts are granted to a business depending on its position on the merchandising chain. Each company in the chain calculates its cost as a percentage of retail.

Cash discounts offer opportunities for cash savings as well as improved cash flow. An efficient method is to pay each invoice just in time for the discount but no sooner. Discounts can be recorded gross or net; the latter method is better for internal control, because any discount not taken when paid is recorded.

7

Long-term
Debt

Long-term debt appears on an organization's balance sheet when the organization has obtained financing of some kind. In general, the larger and more complex the organization, the greater the scale and complexity of financing arrangements. Much material in this chapter, therefore, relates chiefly to large corporate enterprises. But the underlying principles apply to businesses of all kinds.

WHAT IS LONG-TERM DEBT?

By definition, long-term debt—also known as long-term liabilities or noncurrent liabilities—has a maturity, or payable date, more than one year from the balance sheet date. A company takes on long-term debt in order to finance some project or acquisition, such as building a plant or purchasing machinery. A company should always arrange the structuring of long-term debt obligations in consultation with appropriate specialists and professional advisors. There are a variety of forms of long-term debt, each suited to certain specific needs and circumstances. For example, one decision that a company must make when choosing long-term debt as a financing alternative is the date of maturity.

For accounting purposes, it is the maturity that determines whether a debt is short- or long-term. For instance, a company may be planning to retire a debt within the year, but if the due date is more than a year away, it still qualifies as a long-term debt.

Any debt can carry a repayment schedule such that some part of the principal is due within a year from the balance sheet date. In this situation, as mentioned in chapter 6, the amount currently payable is classified under current liabilities, while the noncurrent portion appears in the long-term liabilities section.

Long-term debt may be secured or unsecured. *Secured debt* means that the company has given some form of collateral in order to secure the loan. The creditor can sell off the collateral if the company defaults on the loan. A mortgage loan is a familiar form of secured debt. Unsecured debt, on the other hand, involves no collateral. Unsecured debt has a general claim on a firm's assets that is superior to equity claims but inferior to the claims of secured debt. For this reason, lenders often prefer to make loans secured by collateral.

Sometimes long-term lenders can convert to stockholders of a company. In order to attract investors (and possibly, too, to pay lower interest rates), companies may offer lenders this option. This kind of "convertible" debt, however, remains on the balance sheet as long-term debt until the time of the conversion.

TYPES OF LONG-TERM DEBT

Financing arrangements vary according to the type of borrower, the purpose of the financing, and the nature of the lender. The major categories of long-term debt are loans, lines of credit, mortgages, chattel mortgages, bonds, and convertible debt.

Loans

An unsecured debt based on general credit and involving one borrower and one lender is known simply as a loan. When a company has built up a reputation for creditworthiness, it may be eligible for a loan backed only by its credit rating. Smaller companies arrange such loans directly with their banks or other credit sources. The only obligation of the borrower is to pay interest on the debt as required in the loan document. The document sets forth the identity of the lender and borrower, the amount borrowed, the repayment schedule, the interest rate(s), and the other terms of the loan. The lender states the terms. As time goes by, the lender and the borrower may negotiate modifications to the terms, depending on the status of their relationship, the length of time they have done business together, how previous loans have been serviced, any changes in the condition of the company or the industry, other cash sources now available to the borrower, and so on.

Lines of Credit

Lines of credit are unsecured optional loans, or options to borrow, which may be granted to creditworthy companies. Like an individual with a credit card, a company may choose to use its line of credit, subject to the terms of credit, when and if the need arises. Companies generally use lines of credit as sources of cash to cover short-term cash needs—that is, to bridge any gaps between cash levels and expenditures beyond those levels. A line of credit is a cushion and should not be used to finance longer-term needs, even though it may qualify as a form of long- term debt.

Mortgages

We often speak casually of a "mortgage" as if it were a type of loan, but strictly defined, a *mortgage* is a lien (claim) on property. The borrower gives the lender a claim, or mortgage, on some tangible property. The lender may exercise the claim and obtain the property if the borrower does not repay the loan. If a company obtains money or credit using realty, the loan instrument is called a mortgage or deed of trust. If the collateral is personalty (equipment), the instrument is called a chattel mortgage.

A company may obtain a mortgage loan for either of two reasons. One is to buy realty (a building or other real property). The other is to refinance property to obtain cash. In either case, the evidence of the lien of the lender is a "mortgage payable" document or a trust deed filed in the office of the county recorder in the county where the property is located. And in either case the borrower pays for the title search, title insurance, loan costs, notarization costs, recording fees, and any other costs the lender may require as a condition of the loan. In the event of a default on the loan, the lender can take the property and sell it to satisfy the debt. If the amount realized on the sale is insufficient to pay off the loan, however, the lender may not be able to look to other property owned by the borrower. In this case the lender becomes a general creditor for the unpaid portion of the loan.

In all secured loan transactions, when the borrower has finally paid off the debt, the borrower should see that the lender records proper documents as evidence that the debt has been extinguished. In real property, a notice of reconveyance may be used. It should be recorded in the same office where the original mortgage was recorded, and a copy of the document should be sent to the borrower.

Chattel Mortgages

A company can use a *chattel mortgage* to secure funds to purchase personalty, or equipment. The purchase contract is called a contract of sale or an installment contract. The lender files the chattel mortgage in the office of the county recorder in the county of sale to "give notice to the world" of the debt. In a contract of sale, title does not usually pass to the borrower (the buyer) until all the payments are made as required; in an installment contract, title usually passes to the borrower directly on sale. In either case, the chattel mortgage gives the seller the right to repossess the equipment in the event that the buyer doesn't complete the payments. But chattel mortgages can be hard to enforce. If the borrower moves the equipment to another jurisdiction, it may not be easy for the lender to attach the property to satisfy the debt.

Company books often carry two accounts for real estate mortgage situations: mortgages payable and, perhaps, a deferred interest expense account to cover the many costs of the mortgage loan. In chattel mortgage situations, however, the term may be relatively short. So only one account appears, showing the balance (both principal and interest) due.

Another form of chattel mortgage can involve two or three parties: the borrower, the lender, and sometimes a trustee. Companies use this type of arrangement for the purchase of large assets such as airplanes or railroad cars. The user of the asset is the borrower and arranges the loan terms with a lender such as a bank. Then the user presents a purchase order to the manufacturer of the asset. When the asset is delivered and accepted, the lender pays the manufacturer. The title may go to the lender; or the title may go to a trustee. In the latter event the trustee indicates with a plaque or other distinctive mark that the trustee is the owner of the asset in trust for the lender. The borrower goes ahead and uses the asset, paying the lender over time.

For example, to buy a company automobile, the company selects the car and arranges the financing; the lender makes a check payable to the dealer. In this case, the lender does not use a trustee. The dealer accepts the lender's check, registering the car in the name of the company but showing the lender as the legal owner of the car.

As with a mortgage loan, proper documents should be recorded for a chattel mortgage. And when a loan secured by personalty is paid off, the lender should file a "satisfaction of chattel mortgage" document as proof that the debt no longer exists.

Bonds

When a corporation has need of a large sum of money, long-term debt may take the form of a sale of bonds or debentures. A *bond* may be secured or unsecured; a *debenture* is generally unsecured. Unsecured bonds or debentures are backed by the general credit of the company.

An investor who "buys" a corporate bond or debenture is actually lending money to the corporation. Suppose a company wants to borrow $40 million for 10 years. It can arrange for the sale of 40,000 $1,000 bonds with a 10-year maturity. The company contacts an investment banker to assist in the financing. The investment banker prepares a sales prospectus, giving facts about the corporation, the intended use for the funds, the amount of the borrowing, the interest rate(s), terms of repayment, and other matters of concern to prospective lenders. Usually, some time passes between the corporation's original contact with the investment banker and the sale of the bonds or debentures. Interest rate(s) must be predicted for the date of the sale of the instruments. But few (if any) investment bankers can predict interest rates exactly. Therefore, the bonds or debentures may be sold at a premium, if their interest rate is lower than the prevailing interest rate for like paper on the date of sale. Similarly, if the interest rate on the bonds is higher than the prevailing rate for like paper on the date of sale, the bonds sell at a discount.

The difference between the face amount of a bond and the price the investor pays essentially brings the yield of the bond to the prevailing rate for like paper on the date of sale. For example, if a 10-year $1,000 bond paying 8 percent interest is sold when the prevailing like rate is 7 percent, it will be in great demand, because it will return $80 per year interest compared to $70 for a like instrument. So its price will rise; it will sell at a premium. This bond will sell for around $1,134, and the effect will be that its $80 interest will approximate a 7 percent rate on the $1,134 invested. Or if the prevailing rate is 8.5 percent, this same bond will sell at a discount, for about $941, making the $80 interest roughly equivalent to interest at 8.5 percent.

For purposes of company accounting, a *bond premium*—a price higher than the face value—is like an interest reduction to the company and is earned pro rata over the term of the loan. A *bond discount*, conversely, is like a deferred interest expense and is charged pro rata over the term of the loan. When an investment banker or group sells the bonds, the borrower pays a charge for the sale. This charge is treated like a discount. Premiums, if any, discounts, if any, and charges for the sale of bonds are netted into one account called "premium on loans (or debentures)" or "discount on loans (or debentures)."

Convertible Debt

Convertible debt may originate as unsecured or secured. Originally shown in the long-term debt section of the balance sheet, convertible debt is different from other debt in that it may be converted to equity some time in the future. This option to convert is valuable and is used to attract investors.

Perhaps a corporation wishes to issue bonds to get money for a new plant or working capital. The company expects a good profit, but investors are wary of risk. (In some situations, too, a company may be looking for a way to pay reduced interest rates but may have difficulty finding investors willing to accept low returns.) The solution may be to use convertible debt. The company floats a convertible bond issue, receives the needed money (perhaps at reduced rates), puts it to work as planned, and publicizes its performance.

The investors may now decide to become owners. Convertible bonds give the bondholders the option of surrendering their bonds to the corporation in return for a specified number of shares of stock in the corporation. In this way, the debt is "converted" to equity. When the trade of debt for equity has taken place, the liability is extinguished and the stock accounts are increased. Some lenders, of course, may not want to convert. They can sell their bonds to investors who want the stock, or they will be paid off by the company as the instrument stipulates.

SPECIAL CONSIDERATIONS WITH LONG-TERM DEBT

It is important for the reader of a balance sheet to be aware that long-term debt instruments often contain special covenants or stipulations that affect the company's conduct of its business until the debts are paid. Sometimes these covenants can hamper a company's activities. Footnotes to the financial statements may describe any such special conditions. Without studying the footnotes, it is often hard to assess the full meaning of the company's long-term debt.

A typical covenant might require a company to maintain a certain level of working capital (current assets minus current liabilities). Or the company might be required to maintain a specified "current ratio"—that is, ratio of current assets to current liabilities. Or loan covenants may prohibit the sale of company assets without the lender's approval. These kinds of restrictions are designed to protect the lenders, but they may also prevent a company from taking actions that it normally would or should take.

For example, suppose that under the terms of a loan Acme Containers is forbidden to sell assets. During an analysis of operations, Acme discovers that it is producing certain aluminum containers at a loss. Ordinarily, Acme would cease production of these items and sell off the specialized equipment used to manufacture them. But under the loan covenant, Acme cannot take these steps. It will be necessary for Acme to negotiate a sale of specified assets with the lender to prevent further loss.

OTHER LONG-TERM LIABILITIES

Some kinds of long-term liabilities do not appear on the balance sheet. They include many different types of contractual arrangements between the company and outsiders— arrangements that may limit the company's options to act on its future resources, but which are unrecorded on the company's books until an event occurs in the future. Some of these future events may be such that a company can make a fairly accurate estimate of the long-term liability. Others are such that an accurate estimate is not possible.

In general, for example, leases of all types represent "off-balance-sheet" liabilities. Many businesses lease the premises they occupy. Some leases extend 3 to 5 years into the future, others 25 years or longer. The current portion of rent is a current payable. It is paid as the lease calls for payments—monthly, quarterly, and so on. The rent for the future periods must be paid, but in the future. The company has a certain liability with known due dates. Even so, this liability may not be listed as a long-term liability.

Guarantees or warranties on products sold or services rendered also constitute a type of long-term liability. It can be difficult, however, to show this liability accurately on a balance sheet. A company may have data it can use to determine some amount that may reflect its liability, and perhaps a liability has been set up; but it can be only an estimate. Given the current climate for consumer lawsuits, it may be hard to see the total effect of warranty liabilities. In one actual instance, an automobile long out of the warranty period was rear-ended and burned, and the manufacturer was held liable.

A company may purchase insurance to cover certain losses, but the balance sheet does not spell out the areas of insurance coverage or the limits of coverage. External auditors are not responsible for rating insurance policies. At the same time, insurance is no protection against some kinds of disasters. For example, a San Francisco bread-truck driver ran into a pedestrian, and the pedestrian sued the bread company. The award to the pedestrian was larger than the company's insurance coverage. The company had a long, successful past and good future prospects, but it was forced into bankruptcy.

Other off-balance-sheet factors with possible long-term importance include employee benefits. Businesses are being asked to do more for employees. Employee needs range from day-care centers to training centers to courses in remedial reading, writing, or mathematics. And there have been appeals for benefits such as paternity leave, similar to maternity leave; for medical benefits for persons other than the employee's spouse or children; for additional health and dental benefits. The extent of expenditures for these kinds of benefits over the course of future years may be hard for a company to assess. Yet when a benefit is agreed to, it may very well add significantly to the price of goods sold or services rendered by the company. In effect, it may constitute a long-term liability.

Finally, retired employee benefit costs are not shown on the balance sheet. The costs of health and dental insurance extended to retired employees and their dependents can be large and very difficult to determine. Among other factors, retirees as a group are behaving differently than in earlier decades. Not only are they living longer, but they are moving to new geographical areas, traveling, or taking up new retirement occupations in greater numbers. These activities sometimes entail new sets of risks that affect the company's costs.

To sum up, knowledge of off-balance-sheet liabilities is a necessary ingredient in any assessment of a company's future prospects.

EXAMPLE

Johnson Manufacturing Company Loan Application

Johnson Manufacturing Company makes small engine equipment such as lawn mowers and rototillers. Johnson is a medium-sized company but has visions of competing with the industry giants in domestic and foreign markets. Currently, Johnson needs $50 million to expand its current operations and modernize some of its equipment over the next 2 years. The company expects to benefit from these improvements over the next 7 to 10 years.

Analysts have described Johnson as a "stable" company and the management as "experienced and conservative." The current expansion plans are not representative of past actions, which have been characterized as "slow but steady growth."

You have been hired by Johnson to design a plan to finance the desired expansion and modernization. Using your knowledge of various long-term financing alternatives, and in light of Johnson's balance sheet (example 7.1), discuss the following possibilities:

- Line of credit
- Mortgages
- Convertible debt
- Loan from local bank
- Bond issue

The following information may be useful to you:

1. Johnson has an unsecured line of credit at Friendly Local Bank for $10 million at 16 percent interest.
2. Currently, the prime rate of interest is 12 percent.
3. Current rates for unsecured loans are about 16 percent.
4. Current mortgage rates are 15 percent.
5. Bond issues for similar companies yield 16.5%.
6. The industry average level of long-term debt is 37 percent.
7. In each of the last two years, Johnson has generated a profit of $6.5 million on sales of $290 million.
8. The bank that gave Johnson its long-term debt financing has a first lien on all of the machinery and equipment.

As the balance sheet suggests, Johnson is a healthy and stable firm. Shareholders own about 59 percent of the firm, a strong proportion. Long-term lenders own about 16 percent of the total assets. This company can assume some additional debt. The question is which alternative to use.

Example 7.1

Johnson Manufacturing Company
Statement of Financial Position
Years Ending December 31, 19X4 and 19X3
(numbers in thousands)

	FY19X4	FY 19X3
ASSETS		
Current assets		
Cash	$ 1,826	$ 1,688
Trade accounts receivable	36,816	54,541
Other accounts receivable	626	968
Inventories	160,343	124,349
Prepaid expenses	1,009	1,459
Total current assets	200,620	183,005
Long-lived assets		
Land	960	895
Buildings	40,345	35,879
Machinery and equipment	69,075	61,694
	110,380	98,468
Less depreciation	– 44,450	– 40,359
Net property, plant,		
and equipment	65,930	58,109
Total assets	$266,550	$241,114
LIABILITIES and EQUITY		
Current liabilities		
Notes payable	$ 42,027	$ 1,522
Accounts payable	31,195	33,072
Accrued payroll	11,314	16,619
Accrued interest	1,778	1,917
Taxes	552	3,655
Long-term debt—current	3,973	3,953
Total current liabilities	90,839	60,738
Long-term debt	29,846	39,793
Total liabilities	120,685	100,531
Equity		
Common stock	12,664	12,664
Additional paid capital	54,954	55,619
Retained earnings	78,247	72,300
Total equity	145,865	140,583
Total liabilities and equity	$266,550	$241,114

Line of Credit

In general, lines of credit are not used for long-term financing in healthy companies. Johnson is unlikely to get $50 million in an unsecured discretional line of credit.

Mortgages

A mortgage might be a good alternative here. But Johnson has only $40 million in buildings to pledge (the equipment already has a lien). Perhaps some of the new equipment could be pledged, but then Johnson might find itself unable to sell some of its equipment if it needed to. In addition, a lender would want a pledge with a value in excess of the amount of the loan. In light of all these facts, a mortgage is probably not the best alternative.

Convertible Debt

Convertible debt can serve to lower interest payments and to allow those using the conversion option to participate in future profits generated by the project being financed. But Johnson, being in a strong position, does not need the interest payments lowered. And Johnson's shareholders are unlikely to want to share future profits with anyone.

Loan from Local Bank

An unsecured bank loan is a possibility. However, for a loan of this size, the bank is likely to include so many restrictions in the debt contract that Johnson will not have the freedom it may need in the future. For instance, suppose the contract prohibits the sale of assets. If Johnson's lawn weeder line becomes unprofitable, the company won't be able to sell the equipment and cease production. Clearly, although this restriction may not affect the debt at all, it could be bad for the stockholders.

Bond Issue

This seems the most promising alternative. The issue will raise Johnson's level of long-term debt to about 29 percent, well below the industry average. Profits from current operations will be sufficient to cover the debt expense (assuming that the current profit level continues). And the interest charges are not so high as to be unbearable.

SUMMARY

Long-term debt is debt that is payable more than one year from the balance sheet date. Companies assume long-term debt when they obtain financing for major projects or acquisitions. Long-term debt may be secured—backed by collateral—or unsecured. Unsecured debt includes loans, lines of credit, and some bonds and debentures. Secured debt includes mortgages (on realty) and chattel mortgages (on personalty). Convertible debt, a special category, is debt that may be converted to stockholders' equity at a future date.

It is important to read footnotes to financial statements in order to understand any special covenants on loan instruments that may affect a company's future activities.

Some long-term liabilities do not appear on a balance sheet. These include many contractual arrangements relating to future events; leases, employee benefits, and underinsured losses are some examples.

IV Equity

8

Owners' Equity

Suppose you own a business and you go to a bank for a loan. Sooner or later, the banker is bound to ask about your equity in the business. The banker wants to know what would be left over if you subtracted the dollar amount of your business's total liabilities, as reported on your current balance sheet, from its total assets. Clearly, if that figure were zero—if debt exactly equaled the worth of assets, leaving no equity—you and the banker might have cause for concern. It's also possible for a balance sheet to show disproportionately high equity, a possible clue that invested money is not working hard enough.

Let's look more closely at what owners' equity is and how it is reported in the three forms of organizations: proprietorships, partnerships, and corporations.

WHAT IS OWNERS' EQUITY?

A business owns nothing for itself. The assets of the business belong to its owner(s), whether the business is owned by John Doe or by a hundred thousand stockholders. The liabilities of the business are what the business owes to nonowners. Remember the fundamental accounting equation:

Assets = Liabilities + Equity

This can be restated,

Assets − Liabilities = Equity

Equity, then, is what the business owes to its owner(s) on the date of the balance sheet, once the claims of nonowners have been satisfied.

Although equity is sometimes called "net worth," this term can be misleading. A company is often worth a lot more than the net of its assets minus its liabilities on a particular day. A firm with equity of $500,000 may be "worth" $5 million. One example: As chapter 5 explains, real estate holdings are carried on a company's books at their historical cost. But historical cost of realty often has no relationship to present-day market value. A piece of property listed at its 1970 cost of $100,000 may have a value of $1 million in many U.S. realty markets today—and, incidentally, could cost $1 million to replace.

FORMS OF EQUITY IN DIFFERENT ORGANIZATIONS

Owners' equity basically comes from two sources: invested capital and the earnings of the business. The equity section of the balance sheet for every form of organization shows the beginning owners' equity, the increases from investments, the decreases from withdrawals, the net change due from operations, and the ending owners' equity. The general formula for owners' equity is:

Beginning balance (ending balance at last balance sheet date)

+ Investments by owner(s) during the period
+ Profits for the period (or losses for the period)
- Disinvestments by owner(s) during the period, such as drawings, dividends, or any other withdrawal of assets

= Ending balance (shown on this period's ending balance sheet)

In different kinds of organizations, owners' equity takes somewhat different forms and is reported in different kinds of statements.

Proprietorship

A *proprietorship* (or single proprietorship or sole proprietorship) is an unincorporated business in which an individual owns—and is personally liable for the debts of—the entire enterprise. The owner's personal exposure if the business fails is one major drawback of a proprietorship. There are many advantages, however. All profits belong to the owner, and the owner has complete control over business decisions. Also, this is the easiest kind of organization to form. A proprietorship requires no filing of special papers to start; usually, a person simply notifies the tax, health, and safety authorities, which all businesses have to do. Most local jurisdictions require that a form be filed showing the business name, the owner, and the purpose of the business. Sometimes this information is required to be published in a general circulation newspaper.

The proprietor keeps an equity account in the general ledger. This account shows the beginning owner's equity and how it has changed during the year by the owner's investments or withdrawals and by the business's profits or losses.

In a proprietorship, the owner's equity statement is often included as part of the balance sheet. For example, the equity section of the John Kilgariff Plumbing Company balance sheet looks like this:

John Kilgariff, capital, January 1, 19X3	$ 35,700	
Investments during year	35,000	
Profits for the year	67,500	
	138,200	
Less withdrawals	60,000	
Balance, December 31, 19X3		$78,200

When $78,200 is added to Kilgariff Company's total liabilities, the sum will equal the plumbing company's total assets.

A proprietorship's equity can also be reported in a separate statement, as follows:

John Kilgariff Plumbing Company
Statement of Proprietor's Capital
Year Ended December 31, 19X3

Balance, January 1, 19X3	$ 35,700
Investments during year	35,000
Profits for the year	67,500
	138,200
Less withdrawals	60,000
Balance, December 31, 19X3	$78,200

On Kilgariff's balance sheet, only the last line of the equity statement will appear, like this:

Kilgariff equity December 31, 19X3	$78,200

This equity statement is for a defined period, usually a year, and shows the changes in equity from the beginning to the end of the period. Note that there is no mention of how the investment was made (by cash, equipment, etc.) or of how the disinvestments (withdrawals) were made. Note, too, that Kilgariff's equity statement shows no income taxes due, because a proprietorship is not taxed as a business entity. This is true under the Tax Reform Act of 1986 and has been true for over 50 years of income taxation in this century. As owner of a proprietorship, John Kilgariff files an income statement (Schedule C) as part of his individual federal income tax return and pays income taxes on the profits of the business as part of his personal income.

Partnership

A *partnership* is also unincorporated. In a partnership, two or more persons form a business organization as co-owners to share in profits and losses. Some features make partnerships attractive:

1. A partnership is easy to form. The partners need only to agree to go into business and notify tax, safety, and health authorities that they are going into business. Local jurisdictions usually require the partners to file a form showing the business name, the names of the partners, and the purpose of the business. As with a proprietorship, this information may also be required to be inserted in a general circulation newspaper.

2. The partnership files a federal information income tax return, although the partnership itself is not taxed on its income. Each partner's share of income (or loss) is reported as part of his or her individual income tax return.

There are some features, however, that make a partnership unattractive:

1. There is unlimited liability. If a partnership cannot pay its debts, the partners' personal property can be used to satisfy the partnership debts. And this liability is not necessarily in proportion to the partners' shares. If all the partners but one have no assets outside the partnership, then the one with the assets must pay all the partnership debts up to his or her ability to pay. Thus, one partner with many assets can lose

them all, far beyond what he or she planned to invest. If the partnership is a limited partnership, a person can be a limited partner with explicitly limited liability. It is possible for all partners but one to be limited. But at least one partner must be a general partner and be ready to assume the debts of the partnership.

2. Investments in the partnership, of whatever kind, are lost to the ownership of the investing partner. When investors leave the partnership, they cannot take the specific property they invested but must negotiate a settlement for their interest.

3. Income and losses are not necessarily divided equally among partners. The partners can devise a formula to divide the profits in a way other than equally and can arrange to divide losses differently from profits. Distributions of profits and losses can be made, for example, in proportion to partners' respective contributions to equity.

In view of these features of partnerships, it is always wise to get a lawyer to draw up a partnership agreement. This agreement should state what each person will invest to get the company started, the form and extent of later contributions, the method for participation in profits or losses, the method for valuing the business when a partner wants to leave, and the method for terminating the business and distributing the assets to the partners. The reason this formal document is so important is that it establishes the relationships among the partners in writing. A partner can contribute any or all of the following to a partnership:

1. Cash or other assets, new or used, paid for or not.
2. A personal skill such as sales, marketing, office management, research, or other skills.
3. His or her time.

When the partners may be contributing such unlike assets, crediting each partner a fixed share of the profits is not always equitable. One method of recognizing these different contributions is to give each partner a fair return on his or her average capital investment, then a fair return for his or her skill and time, then distributing the remainder on some set percentage basis or equally.

A partnership equity statement, showing changes in equity from the last balance sheet to the present, can be shown as part of the balance sheet. Catalli & Paalman Hardware provides an example:

	A. J. Catalli	L. Paalman	Total	
Balance, January 1	$130,400	$142,100	$272,500	
Investments during year	10,000	_____	10,000	
Profits for the year	57,500	55,000	112,500	
	197,900	197,100	395,000	
Less withdrawals	54,000	48,000	102,000	
Balance, December 31	$143,900	$149,100		$293,000

When Catalli & Paalman Company's total liabilities and the $293,000 owners' equity are added together, they will equal the total assets of the hardware company.

A partnership's changes in equity may also be shown in a separate statement. In this case, only the total end-of-year equity appears on the balance sheet. A typical separate equity statement for a partnership is:

Catalli & Paalman Hardware
Statement of Partners' Capital
Year Ended December 31, 19X5

	A. J. Catalli	L. Paalman	Total
Balance, January 1	$130,400	$142,100	$272,500
Investments during year	10,000	_____	10,000
Profit for the year	57,500	55,000	112,500
	197,900	197,100	395,000
Less withdrawals	54,000	48,000	102,000
Balance, December 31	$143,900	$149,100	$293,000

In both forms of partnership owners' equity statement, note the split between the two partners of the $112,500 total profit for the year. Catalli and Paalman have agreed to a formula that developed these respective shares. Each partner's share represents a return on the capital he invested, compensation for his skill and time, and an additional amount calculated according to an agreed-to profit-sharing ratio. However, Catalli and Paalman are free to arrange an entirely different formula for distributing losses in bad years if they wish to do so.

Corporation

In a corporation, the equity section of the balance sheet can show many more types of equity than in a proprietorship or a partnership. A *corporation* is an incorporated legal and taxable entity separate from its owners (stockholders). A corporation may be owned by one or more persons. If the business follows a prescribed procedure for incorporation required by the state and if the state charters the corporation, it is called a "de jure corporation." If the business does not follow the procedure required by the state but presents itself as a corporation and acts like one, it is called a "de facto corporation." (A de facto corporation should file the proper papers to become a de jure corporation.)

In many ways, a corporation is treated as a person. It can do business, make sales and purchases, and receive and disburse money in its own name. Like an individual, a corporation can commit criminal acts, such as price fixing or polluting the environment. And a corporation can be convicted for these crimes, although obviously it cannot be sent to jail. Usually, in criminal proceedings, the corporation and the responsible officers become co-defendants. In the event the defense loses, the corporation may pay a fine, and the officers may pay a fine and/or go to prison.

Because the corporation is considered a separate legal entity, the federal government taxes its income at corporate tax rates. Many states also tax corporations on their income, and some states collect a minimum tax—a tax payable whether or not the corporation has taxable income for the year.

Most large businesses in the United States today are corporations, because the corporate form of organization offers certain unique advantages for large-scale operations. Some of these advantages have a direct bearing on owners' equity. For example, in a commercial corporation the owners' liability is limited strictly to their investment. The corporation is deemed separate from the owners, so creditors can look only to the assets of the corporation to satisfy any amounts owed, not to the personal assets of the owners. This protection for the owner is called the "corporate veil." (This protection does not extend to professionals such as doctors who incorporate their practices for ease in transferring interests of ownership, because in such a case the doctor himself or herself is the business.)

Also, a corporation has the potential to gather together great amounts of capital. By selling shares of stock, a corporation can attract thousands of investors. Owners of stock in a corporation have liability limited to the amount of their investment; they can transfer their investment if they desire; and by making a modest investment they can benefit from participation in a business with professional management and an ongoing existence. For these and other reasons, corporate stocks are attractive investments.

Stockholders' (or shareholders') investment, plus the corporation's retained earnings, constitute the equity amounts shown on a corporate balance sheet.

Types of Stock

In a corporation there must be at least one class of stock, called *common stock*. There may also be other kinds, called *preferred stock*. Common stockholders have the right to vote at annual meetings, while preferred stockholders generally do not. Also, common stockholders may receive higher *divi-*

dends (distributions of profits) as profits rise, while preferred stockholders are generally paid dividends at a fixed predetermined rate. On the other hand, if a time comes when the corporation can't pay dividends to everybody, preferred stockholders get paid first; common stockholders may receive reduced dividends or none at all. And in the event of liquidation of the corporation, once creditors have been paid, preferred stockholders take precedence over common stockholders to receive shares of the assets—hence the designation "preferred."

Each class of stock is shown separately in the balance sheet's equity section. Stock can be par value, meaning that its price is printed on the certificate, or no-par value, with no price printed on the certificate. The secretary of state of the state in which the corporation is approved will authorize the number of shares requested for each class. When the shares of stock are initially sold to an investor, a certificate of shares is made out in his or her name. (Often, of course, the investor is an organization such as a pension fund, university, or mutual fund.) This is called issued stock. A company may sell only the authorized number of shares, but on application, the secretary of state may authorize more shares.

Treasury stock is issued stock of the corporation that the corporation has reacquired by purchase or by some other means and has not canceled. It is usually shown at the end of the equity section as a reduction to equity. Any changes in treasury stock amounts may be footnoted. Treasury stock is in a kind of accounting limbo. While it has been issued and not canceled, it nevertheless does not receive dividends, cannot be voted, and does not represent ownership.

Premium or Discount on Stock

If the amount a corporation receives for its original issue of par value stock is equal to the par value, then that amount becomes the invested capital. Sometimes the amount received is above the par value; the excess is called a *premium on stock* and may be listed on a balance sheet as "additional paid-in capital." The invested capital is then shown in two amounts, as the par value of the stock sold and as the premium. If the amount received for the original issue is below the par value, the stock was sold at a discount. The invested capital is shown in two accounts, as the par value of the stock sold and as the *discount on stock*. In this case, the discount is a debit to be subtracted from the stock account. The premium or discount on stock is a modifier account to the class to which it relates and is carried on the books and shown on the balance sheet.

Stock sold below par value may create a stockholders' liability for the difference between par and the amount paid. For instance, stock in PDQ Corporation has a par value of $2.50. Mr. Green buys 100 shares at $2.00 per share. If the company goes bankrupt, Mr. Green may have a liability for $50 (100 x $ .50).

When stock issued at par value is converted to no-par stock, the premium or discount is merged into the par value. The amount received for the original issue of par value stock is the invested capital of the no-par stock.

In a corporation there are accounts for each class of stock and its premium or discount, and there are accounts for each class of treasury stock. There is usually very little change in these accounts. If changes do occur, footnotes explain any differences between the beginning and the end of the year.

For example, if a corporation's stock were originally issued at a premium, the equity section of the balance sheet would show:

Common stock (10,000 shares authorized at 100 par per share; 9,000 shares issued)	900,000	
Premium on common stock	20,000	920,000

If the stock were converted to no-par stock, the balance sheet would show:

Common stock (10,000 shares authorized, 9,000 shares issued)	920,000

If the stock were originally issued at a discount, the equity section of the balance sheet would show:

Common stock (10,000 shares authorized, 8,000 shares issued)	800,000	
Less discount on common stock	25,000	775,000

If this stock were converted to no-par stock, the equity section would show:

Common stock (10,000 shares authorized, 8,000 shares issued)	775,000

Changes in the stock amount are footnoted as they occur. For example:

Common no-par stock (10,000 shares authorized, 9,300 shares issued)[1]	892,450

1. 875 shares were sold in 19X5 for $86,700.

Retained Earnings

The *retained earnings* component of a corporate equity statement measures the undistributed profits of the corporation.

A corporation's profits from operations are recorded in the retained earnings account. From this account dividends are declared, not paid, and created as liabilities to be paid at a later date. From this account federal and state income taxes payable are recognized, not paid, and created as liabilities to be paid later.

The credit balance in the retained earnings account may be reduced by an appropriation for a valid corporate purpose. The *appropriation,* an amount expressed in dollars, is part of retained earnings but is restricted, or "set aside" for a specific purpose. Appropriations are usually described by purpose, such as "Appropriation for purchase of treasury stock," or "Appropriations for purchase of land for new plant." Appropriations do not, however, represent actual cash set aside.

It is only in the retained earnings section of a corporation's equity statement that there are many changes. Among these changes may be an increase due to the year's net profit (or a decrease due to the year's net loss); decreases due to dividends declared; and decreases due to income taxes incurred on profits, if any. Changes internal to retained earnings are increases to, or decreases of, appropriations. Because the retained earnings account has many transactions that affect it, a separate statement is shown, called the "statement of retained earnings." This statement details how retained earnings have changed since the last balance sheet.

The retained earnings statement of the Jopsim Corporation (see page 146) reflects typical changes in retained earnings from one year's end to the next. The final figure for total retained earnings at the end of the current year will be entered in the stockholders' equity section of the corporation's balance sheet, with a note such as "see separate statement."

EXAMPLES

Based upon your reading of this chapter, draft a statement of equity for each of the following scenarios.

Proprietorship

Leo Pierson is sole proprietor of Pierson Company. At the beginning of the year 19X6, he had $145,000 equity. During the year, he invested an additional $10,000 in the business. At the end of the year, the company realized profits of $87,000. Over the course of the year, Pierson made withdrawals totaling $60,000. What will his equity statement look like

Jopsim Corporation
Retained Earnings Statement
Year Ended December 31, 19X6

UNAPPROPRIATED:			
Balance, January 1		$516,000	
Earnings during year		127,000	
From appropriation for plant site purchase		200,000	
Dividends declared	$100,000	843,000	
To appropriation for treasury stock purchases	50,000	150,000	
Balance, December 31			$693,000
APPROPRIATED:			
For plant site purchase, January 1	$200,000		
To unappropriated	200,000		
Balance, December 31		—	
For treasury stock purchase, January 1	$75,000		
From unappropriated	50,000		
Balance, December 31		$125,000	
Balance, December 31			$125,000
Total Retained Earnings, December 31			$918,000

as a part of the balance sheet? As a separate statement of owner's equity?

Example 8.1 shows how the statement should be drawn up as part of the balance sheet; example 8.2 as a separate statement.

Partnership

Rose Paulsen and James Scatena are partners in Paulsen & Scatena, Architects. At the beginning of 19X7, they had equity of $176,000 and $147,000, respectively, for a total

Example 8.1

Mr. Pierson, Equity (or Net Worth)

Balance, January 1, 19X6	$145,000	
Investments	10,000	
Profits for year 19X6	87,000	
	242,000	
Less drawings	60,000	
		$182,000

Example 8.2

Pierson Company
Statement of Owner's Equity
December 31, 19X6

Balance, January 1, 19X6	$145,000
Investments	10,000
Profit for year 19X6	87,000
	242,000
Less drawings	60,000
Balance, December 31, 19X6	$182,000

---

equity of $323,000. During the year, Scatena made a $20,000 contribution to the company. The firm realized profits of $163,000, which were split 56.44 percent to Paulsen and 43.56 percent to Scatena. Each partner also withdrew $60,000 over the course of the year.

First draw up the partners' equity statement as part of the firm's balance sheet. It should resemble example 8.3.

Now show Paulsen and Scatena's equity as a separate statement of partners' capital; see example 8.4.

Corporation

The equity section of the balance sheet of Jopsim Company, Inc. includes not only preferred and common stock but re-

Example 8.3

Partners' Equity

	R. Paulsen	J. Scatena	Total
Balance, January 1	$176,000	$147,000	$323,000
Investment	——	20,000	20,000
Profit for year	92,000	71,000	163,000
	268,000	238,000	506,000
Less drawings	60,000	60,000	120,000
	$208,000	$178,000	
			$386,000

---

tained earnings. Start by putting together the retained earnings figures. Jopsim began the year 19X5 with $1,211,677 in retained earnings, realized $306,652 in profits in 19X5, and distributed dividends totaling $148,228 in 19X5. Your statement of retained earnings for Jopsim should match example 8.5.

Now compile Jopsim's stockholders' equity section. Jopsim received authorization to issue 100,000 shares of preferred stock with a par value of $10 per share. It had issued 99,150

Example 8.4

Paulsen & Scatena, Architects
Statement of Partners' Capital
Year Ended December 31, 19X7

	R. Paulsen	J. Scatena	Total
Balance, January 1	$176,000	$147,000	$323,000
Investment	——	20,000	20,000
Profit for year	92,000	71,000	163,000
	268,000	238,000	506,000
Less drawings	60,000	60,000	120,000
Balance	$208,000	$178,000	$386,000

Example 8.5

Jopsim Company, Inc.
Statement of Retained Earnings
Year Ended December 31, 19X5

Balance, January 1	$1,211,677
Earnings for the year	306,652
	1,518,329
Less dividends declared	148,228
Balance, December 31	$1,370,101

---

of these shares in previous years and received, in addition to
the par value, a premium totaling $8,260. The remaining 850
shares were sold at par during the year. Jopsim was authorized to sell 20,000 shares of $10 par value common stock,
which sold (at a premium) for $210,000 in previous years.
Add to these amounts the end-of-year balance from the retained earnings statement (example 8.5), and you should have
a stockholders' equity statement much like example 8.6.

SUMMARY

Equity is what a business owes to its owner(s) at the balance
sheet date, once the superior claims of nonowners have been
satisfied. Equity may also be called net worth, net assets, or
capital. There are two basic sources of equity: invested capital
and the earnings of the business. The balance sheet for every
form of organization shows the beginning owners' equity, the
investments and withdrawals made, the net change from
operations, and the ending owners' equity.

A proprietorship is an unincorporated enterprise owned by
one person. The equity statement can be part of the balance
sheet or can be a separate statement.

A partnership, also unincorporated, is owned by more than
one person. The owners' personal assets may be at risk, but a

Example 8.6

Stockholders' Equity

Preferred stock (100,000 shares, par value $10, authorized and issued)[1]	$1,000,000
Premium on preferred stock	8,260
Common stock (20,000 shares, par value $10, authorized and issued)	200,000
Premium on common stock	10,000
Retained earnings (see statement)	1,370,101
Total stockholders' equity	$2,588,361

---

1. During the year, the remaining 850 shares of preferred stock were sold at par.

limited partnership can protect all but one partner. The equity statement can be part of the balance sheet or can be separate.

A corporation can be owned by one or more persons. It is incorporated; that is, it exists as a legal entity apart from its owners. Corporate owners' equity consists of stockholders' invested capital plus the corporation's undistributed retained earnings. Types of stock include common stock, preferred stock, and treasury stock; separate accounts are also kept for premiums or discounts on stock in each class. Retained earnings accounts undergo changes due to dividends declared, profits realized, taxes incurred, and so on; retained earnings can also be adjusted by appropriations.

Analyzing Financial Statements

9

Analyzing Financial Ratios

Company managers, investment bankers, Wall Street brokers, accountants, and individual investors are a few of the kinds of people who study the numbers on the financial statements of companies. Taken by themselves, however, these numbers can be fairly unrevealing. What do they say about a company's ability to pay its bills? About the company's level of indebtedness compared to that of its competition? About the company's efficiency in the use of assets? To unlock the meanings of the numbers on financial statements, analysts have developed numerous comparative measures, generally referred to as ratios.

Used against a backdrop of information about an industry and its worldwide business environment, financial ratios can be helpful tools. But financial ratios are not magic. It takes a lot of practice to be able to make effective use of them. Also, no one ratio is equally applicable to all situations. Things change from year to year and from industry to industry. The past is never a sure guide to the future. Still, when you've had some experience working with ratios as analytical tools, you will find that you'll gain a sharper eye for business patterns, problems, and promising situations.

WHAT ARE FINANCIAL RATIOS?

A *ratio* is an expression of the relationship of one number to another. The relationship of 1 to 3, for example, can be expressed as the ratio "1 to 3" or "1:3." It can also be expressed as 1 ÷ 3, or 1/3, or .333, or 33.3 percent, or 33 1/3 percent. Ratios are often expressed as decimals or percentages.

Ratios provide a way of making financial statements comparable, both within a company and among companies. For example, we can compare Mammoth Widget's ratio of current assets to current liabilities this year to the same ratio last year. We can also compare Mammoth's ratio to that of other widget companies, both larger and smaller than Mammoth. And perhaps we can compare Mammoth's ratio to the industry-wide statistical norm for widget manufacturers over a span of years.

One of the most basic, and probably one of the most useful, tools of ratio analysis is the "common size statement." A common size statement presents every item as a percentage of the largest item on the statement. A balance sheet can be turned into a common size statement; so can an income statement.

For example, the largest item on Mammoth Widget's income statement is sales, and all other items can be expressed as percentages of the sales figure, as in this highly condensed income statement:

	Dollar amounts	Common size percentages
Sales	$100,000	100%
Cost of goods sold	30,000	30
Gross profit	70,000	70
Operating expenses	54,000	54
Net income	$16,000	16%

Common size percentages clarify the relationships among the statement's components, facilitating comparisons between two years or between two companies in the same year. For example, if Mammoth's net income remains in the 16 percent range for several years and then drops to 12 percent, someone should ask what happened. On the other hand, if Mammoth's competitor, Colossal Widget, has very similar common size percentages in all categories except one—say, a net income of 8 percent—Colossal may want to look at its own operations.

There are three other general groups of ratios:

1. Liquidity and turnover ratios measure a company's ability to meet current obligations on time and to use assets efficiently.

2. Leverage or solvency ratios measure the degree to which the company has obtained financing by using funds of nonowners as opposed to using funds of owners (investors).

3. Profitability ratios measure a company's efficiency in generating sales and controlling expenses, as reflected in net profits.

These types of ratios are widely used in management decision making and financial analysis. In the brief discussions that follow, I will not attempt to encompass all the ratios in use but will offer some typical examples.

Note that many of the ratios use averages. For example, the raw material inventory turnover ratio uses the year's beginning value of raw materials plus the ending value, divided by two for an average value.

LIQUIDITY AND TURNOVER RATIOS

Liquidity and turnover ratios all have to do with current assets. Liquidity ratios measure a company's ability to pay current debts on the basis of current assets. Turnover ratios (or activity ratios) assess the movement of the company's current assets.

Current Ratio

What is a comfortable amount of working capital? The current ratio is often a more helpful measure of short-term financial strength or liquidity than the dollar amount of working capital. This ratio measures how many times current assets can pay current liabilities. The current ratio can be expressed as "2:1, "3.1:1," and so on. The larger the first number, the greater the asset strength. And while there are many exceptions, analysts generally say that, as a rough rule of thumb, a 2:1 current ratio is a minimum requirement.

$$\text{Current ratio} = \frac{\text{Current assets}}{\text{Current liabilities}}$$

Case A: Current ratio $= \dfrac{\$56,000}{\$28,000} = 2\text{:}1 \text{ or } 2.0$

Case B: Current ratio $= \dfrac{\$90,000}{\$30,000} = 3\text{:}1 \text{ or } 3.0$

Composition of Current Ratio

By studying the composition of current ratio, we can see what assets are needed to pay off all current liabilities, starting with the most liquid. The composition of current ratio is a series of cumulative measures of assets ranked by liquidity and divided by current liabilities. By comparing this year's data with last year's, management may be able to detect potentially significant changes in asset composition. Examples of composition of current ratio data are:

	19X3			19X2		
	Amount	Ratio	Cumu-lative	Amount	Ratio	Cumu-lative
Cash	$22,000	0.44	.44	$ 20,000	0.33	.33
Accounts receivable	63,000	1.26	1.70	40,000	.67	1.00
Inventories	23,000	.46	2.16	40,000	.67	1.67
Prepaid expenses	2,000	.04	2.20	2,000	.03	1.70
Total current assets	$110,000			$102,000		
Total current liabilities	$ 50,000			$ 60,000		

Acid Test Ratio

The acid test ratio or quick ratio measures how many times current assets *less inventories* can pay current liabilities. The acid test ratio excludes inventories because inventories must be sold before they can be used to settle liabilities. The acid test ratio is a more demanding test of financial strength than the current ratio. It is expressed as "1:1," "1.5:1," and so on. The larger the first number, the greater the strength. The often-cited (though not always applicable) rule of thumb for the acid test ratio is that 1:1 is minimum.

$$\text{Acid test ratio} = \frac{\text{Current assets} - \text{Inventories}}{\text{Current liabilities}}$$

Case A: Acid test ratio $= \dfrac{\$56,000 - \$14,000}{\$28,000} = 1.5:1$

Case B: Acid test ratio $= \dfrac{\$90,000 - \$30,000}{\$30,000} = 2:1$

Accounts Receivable Turnover (ART)

This ratio measures the relationship between sales on account and average receivables and is expressed as a number. The higher the number, the better the collection effort.

$$\text{ART} = \frac{\text{Sales on account during period}}{(\text{Beginning accounts receivable} + \text{Ending accounts receivable})/2}$$

Case: $\text{ART} = \dfrac{\$500,000}{(\$54,000 + \$46,000)/2} = 10$

Collection Period for Accounts Receivable (CPAR)

The CPAR uses the accounts receivable turnover number from the preceding ratio to measure how long a company is taking to collect accounts receivable. CPAR is measured in days and expressed as a number. The lower the number, the better.

$$\text{CPAR} = \frac{360}{\text{Accounts receivable turnover}}$$

Case A: $\text{CPAR} = \dfrac{360}{10} = 36 \text{ days}$

Case B: $\text{CPAR} = \dfrac{360}{12} = 30 \text{ days}$

Inventory Turnover

The inventory turnover ratio measures how many times a merchandiser's average inventory was sold during the year, expressed as a number. The higher the number, the more efficient was the use of inventory in sales.

$$\text{Inventory turnover} = \frac{\text{Cost of goods sold during period}}{(\text{Beginning inventory} + \text{Ending inventory})/2}$$

Case A: Inventory turnover $= \dfrac{\$300{,}000}{(\$120{,}000 + \$80{,}000)/2} = 3$

Case B: Inventory turnover $= \dfrac{\$400{,}000}{(\$120{,}000 + \$80{,}000)/2} = 4$

Raw Material Inventory Turnover

Raw material inventory turnover measures how many times a manufacturer's average raw material inventory was used during the year; it is expressed as a number. The higher the number, the more efficient the use of raw materials.

Raw material inventory turnover =
$$\frac{\text{Raw material inventory used}}{(\text{Beginning} + \text{Ending raw material inventory})/2}$$

Case A: Raw material inventory turnover =
$$\frac{\$200{,}000}{(\$56{,}000 + \$44{,}000)/2} = \frac{\$200{,}000}{\$50{,}000} = 4$$

Case B: Raw material inventory turnover =
$$\frac{\$300{,}000}{(\$56{,}000 + \$66{,}000)/2} = \frac{\$300{,}000}{\$60{,}000} = 5$$

Accounts Payable Turnover (APT)

The APT ratio measures the relationship between purchases on account and the average payables. Used in conjunction with the PPAP (see below), APT provides management with a rough guide by which to measure payments taking cash discounts. This ratio is not, however, as precise a method of control as recording invoices net, as recommended in chapter 6. The APT is expressed as a number; the higher the number, the better.

$$\text{APT} = \frac{\text{Purchases on account during period}}{(\text{Beginning accounts payable} + \text{Ending accounts payable})/2}$$

Case A: $APT = \dfrac{\$200,000}{(\$6,000 + \$4,000)/2} = 40$

Case B: $APT = \dfrac{\$104,500}{(\$8,300 + 10,700)/2} = 11$

Payment Period for Accounts Payable (PPAP)

The PPAP measures the average age in days of accounts payable at payment date. It should approximate the first discount date given in the credit terms; for example, 30 if the terms are 2/30, n/60. The formula incorporates the APT number from the preceding ratio:

$$PPAP = \frac{360}{APT}$$

Case A: $PPAP = \dfrac{360}{40} = 9$ days (terms 1/10, n/30)

Case B: $PPAP = \dfrac{360}{11} = 32.7$ days (terms 2/30, 1/60, n/90)

LEVERAGE RATIOS

Sometimes called solvency or overall debt and equity ratios, the ratios that follow (and others) are used as a group to indicate the size of creditors' claims on assets relative to owners' claims on assets. Too much long-term debt can be risky both for a company's stockholders and for its creditors.

Debt Ratio

The debt ratio indicates overall debt capitalization; that is, nonowners' claims on assets as a proportion of total assets. This ratio is expressed as a percentage, calculated by the formula:

$$\text{Debt ratio} = \frac{\text{Total liabilities}}{\text{Total assets}}$$

Creditors look for a low debt-to-asset ratio to protect themselves. Owners tend to prefer a high ratio.

Long-term Debt Ratio

The long-term debt ratio takes the debt ratio a step further. This ratio measures against total assets the long-term debt of the company, to show how much of the value of the company's assets is financed with long-term debt.

$$\text{Long-term debt ratio} = \frac{\text{Long-term debt}}{\text{Total assets}}$$

Equity Ratio

The equity (or net worth) ratio indicates how much of the value of a company's assets is capitalized by invested capital, including both common and preferred stocks.

$$\text{Equity ratio} = \frac{\text{Total equity}}{\text{Total assets}}$$

Common Equity Ratio

The common equity ratio refines the equity ratio by including only the value of common stock.

$$\text{Common equity ratio} = \frac{\text{Common equity}}{\text{Total assets}}$$

Times Interest Earned (TIE)

The TIE ratio is a measure of a company's ability to pay finance charges (interest on debt). The TIE helps managers and analysts foresee just how burdensome these predictable periodic payments will be. It is based on net operating income from the income statement.

$$\text{TIE ratio} = \frac{\text{Net operating income}}{\text{Total interest expense}}$$

PROFITABILITY RATIOS

Profitability ratios as a group use figures from the company's income statement to measure management's success in obtaining desired returns relative to various components of the business—return relative to total sales, return relative to capital invested, and so forth.

Gross Profit Ratio

Operating Income Ratio

Net Profit Ratio

These three ratios, expressed as percentages, provide different measures of profitability of sales. The gross profit margin, or gross profit percentage, gives an average profit margin on all products sold before all selling and administrative expenses. The operating income margin shows profit before taxes (in a corporation) relative to total sales. Finally, the net profit ratio shows profitability relative to total sales after all expenses and federal taxes. When compared with a company's own margins in other years and with margins in competing companies, these margins can suggest how well management is performing.

$$\text{Gross profit margin} = \frac{\text{Gross profit}}{\text{Net sales}}$$

Case A: $\text{Gross profit margin} = \frac{\$240,000}{\$1,200,000} = 20.0\%$

Case B: $\text{Gross profit margin} = \frac{\$120,000}{\$360,000} = 33.3\%$

$$\text{Operating income margin} = \frac{\text{Operating income}}{\text{Net sales}}$$

Case A: Operating income margin $= \dfrac{\$96,000}{\$1,200,000} = 8.0\%$

Case B: Operating income margin $= \dfrac{\$30,000}{\$360,000} = 8.3\%$

$$\text{Net profit margin} = \frac{\text{After-tax net income}}{\text{Net sales}}$$

Case A: Net profit margin $= \dfrac{\$30,000}{\$1,200,000} = 2.5\%$

Case B: Net profit margin $= \dfrac{\$16,000}{\$360,000} = 4.4\%$

Return on Total Assets (RTA)

The RTA measures how effectively a company's average assets are being used. This ratio is expressed as a decimal or a percentage; the higher the figure, the better. As you know, however, assets can be understated, because the company's balance sheet may not reflect increases in the value of long-lived assets. If this increased value is not recorded, assets appear lower, making the RTA percentage higher.

$$RTA = \frac{\text{Net income for the period}}{(\text{Beginning assets} - \text{Ending assets})/2}$$

Case A: RTA $= \dfrac{\$125,000}{(\$550,000 + \$450,000)/2} = 0.25 \text{ or } 25\%$

Case B: RTA $= \dfrac{\$150,000}{(\$550,000 + \$450,000)/2} = 0.30 \text{ or } 30\%$

Return on Equity (ROE)

Return on Common Equity (ROCE)

Return on equity (or return on net worth) and return on common equity ratios measure how effectively management is using the owners' investment. These ratios are expressed as decimals or percentages; the higher, the better. Again, as equity can be understated because of increased value of long-lived assets, these ratios become higher if the current market value of the assets is not booked.

In a corporation, the return on common equity ratio (ROCE) is a more important measure than return on total equity. As mentioned in chapter 8, preferred stockholders get only pre-determined dividends. Return on common equity, therefore, removes the effect of preferred stock dividends from income, then measures the balance against common stockholders' equity.

$$\text{Return on equity} = \frac{\text{Net income of the period}}{(\text{Beginning equity} + \text{Ending equity})/2}$$

$$\textbf{Case A: } \text{ROE} = \frac{\$100,000}{(\$290,000 + \$410,000)/2} = 28.6 \text{ or } 28.6\%$$

$$\textbf{Case B: } \text{ROE} = \frac{\$150,000}{(\$430,000 + \$500,000)/2} = 32.3 \text{ or } 32.3\%$$

$$\text{ROCE} = \frac{\text{Net income of the period} - \text{Preferred dividends of period}}{(\text{Beginning common equity} + \text{Ending common equity})/2}$$

$$\textbf{Case A: } \text{ROCE} = \frac{\$100,000}{(\$240,000 + \$360,000)/2} = 33.3\%$$

$$\textbf{Case B: } \text{ROCE} = \frac{\$150,000}{(\$250,000 + \$400,000)/2} = 46.15\%$$

EXAMPLE

Alpha Manufacturing Ratio Analysis

Alpha Manufacturing & Sales Corporation designs, manufactures, and sells building, industrial, and defense products involving application of their patented metalworking technological innovations. They are highly diversified, selling products in home appliance, auto parts, and defense markets.

You are in charge of a large pension fund. In order to decide whether or not Alpha is a safe, sound investment, you embark upon an analysis of some key ratios. You are provided with Alpha's 19X8 and 19X9 balance sheets and income statements (example 9.1). You're aware of some facts about the industry as a whole; for instance, the long-term debt ratio for the industry averages 39 percent. You are also aware that you'd need more information than these statements provide in order to do a full assessment—and that there are no hard-and-fast rules about what is desirable or undesirable for a given ratio. For example, a high percentage of shareholders' equity may be desirable from the shareholders' standpoint (it gives them more power), but it may not be the optimum situation for the company.

Using the formulas given in this chapter, compile the following ratios for Alpha's fiscal 19X8 and 19X9:

- Current ratio
- Acid test ratio
- Accounts receivable turnover
- Average collection period
- Inventory turnover
- Debt ratio
- Long-term debt ratio
- Equity ratio

- Times interest earned
- Gross profit ratio
- Operating profit ratio
- Net profit ratio
- Return on total assets
- Return on equity

Your results should look like the list in example 9.2. As you survey these figures, how do you think Alpha looks in each area?

Example 9.1

Alpha Manufacturing & Sales Corporation
Statement of Financial Position
December 31
(in thousands)

	19X8	19X9
ASSETS		
Cash	$ 3,344	$ 7,302
Accounts receivable (net)	110,719	120,960
Inventories	142,089	131,209
Prepaid expenses	11,282	9,077
Total current assets	267,434	268,548
Land	15,202	15,733
Buildings	59,038	73,020
Machinery, equipment, etc.	184,277	207,024
Construction in progress	13,886	13,754
	272,403	309,531
Less accumulated depreciation	132,856	150,371
Total PP&E (net)	139,547	159,160
Special tooling (net)	5,409	4,205
Leases and contracts received	15,820	16,158
Goodwill	9,655	9,351
Other	3,461	11,325
Total Assets	$441,326	$468,747

Example 9.1 (continued)

LIABILITIES AND EQUITY		
Accounts payable	$49,241	$56,691
Unsecured notes payable	5,127	0
Accrued expenses:		
Salaries and wages	12,190	12,440
Withheld taxes	11,106	14,683
Other	12,518	11,197
Current portion—long-term debt	18,931	10,058
Income taxes	15,308	9,936
Total current liabilities	124,421	115,005
Deferred compensation	9,863	12,073
Long-term debt	112,594	129,118
Total long-term liabilities	122,457	141,191
Total liabilities	246,878	256,196
Common stock	106,599	112,073
Paid-in capital	11,240	11,240
Retained earnings	76,609	89,238
Total equity	194,448	212,551
Total Liabilities and Equity	$441,326	$468,747

Alpha Manufacturing & Sales Corporation
Statement of Income
Year Ended December 31

	19X8	19X9
Sales	$1,347,896	$1,489,388
Cost of sales	1,057,996	1,115,350
Gross profit	289,900	374,038
Selling and advertising	58,573	72,014
General and administrative	57,192	71,292
Total operating expenses	115,765	143,306
Operating profit	174,135	230,732
Other income and expense:		
Interest	(3,560)	(3,531)
Other (net)	(202)	490
Total	(3,762)	(3,041)
Income before taxes	170,373	227,691
Income taxes	68,149	90,825
Net Income after Taxes	$ 102,224	$ 136,866

Example 9.2

	19X8	19X9
Current ratio:		
$\dfrac{267,434}{124,421}\quad\dfrac{268,548}{115,005}$	2.15	2.34
Acid test ratio:		
$\dfrac{113,063}{124,421}\quad\dfrac{128,262}{115,005}$	0.91	1.12
Accounts receivable turnover: Do not have figures for sales on account. Do not have ending 19X7 accounts receivable.	―	―
Average collection period: Cannot develop accounts receivable turnover.	―	―
Inventory turnover: $\dfrac{1,057,996}{(142,089+131,209)/2}$ Do not have ending 19X7 inventory.	―	7.72
Debt ratio:		
$\dfrac{246,878}{441,326}\quad\dfrac{256,196}{468,747}$	0.56	0.55
Long-term debt ratio:		
$\dfrac{112,457}{441,326}\quad\dfrac{141,191}{468,747}$	0.28	0.30
Equity ratio:		
$\dfrac{194,448}{441,326}\quad\dfrac{212,551}{468,747}$	0.44	0.45
Times interest earned:		
$\dfrac{174,135}{3,560}\quad\dfrac{230,732}{3,531}$	48.91	65.34
Gross profit ratio:		
$\dfrac{289,900}{1,347,896}\quad\dfrac{374,038}{1,489,388}$	21.51	25.11
Operating profit ratio:		
$\dfrac{174,135}{1,374,896}\quad\dfrac{230,732}{1,489,388}$	12.67	15.49

Example 9.2 (continued)

	19X8	19X9
Net profit ratio:		
102,224 136,866	7.44	9.19
1,374,896 1,489,388		
Return on total assets:		
102,224		
(441,326 + 468,747)/2	——	22.47
Do not have ending 19X7 total assets.		
Return on equity:		
102,224		
(194,448 + 212,551)/2	——	50.23
Do not have ending 19X7 equity.		

In the first group of ratios, liquidity and turnover ratios, it appears that Alpha is highly liquid—a very strong prospect for the short term, at least—and that assets are moving at desirable rates.

In terms of leverage, the second group, Alpha has a manageable level of debt. Indeed, since industry average for long-term debt is 39 percent, Alpha could probably afford a bit more than its current level of 21.8 percent. Its TIE shows its capacity to make interest payments over the long term; 64.305 is a strong figure, indicating that profits can comfortably absorb debt service. Owners' equity at 57 percent is also satisfactory.

Finally, profitability looks good. By any standard, a 22.9 percent return on assets and 40.3 percent return on equity suggest that Alpha's earnings are strong.

SUMMARY

Financial ratios provide a way to compare and interpret balance sheet and income statement numbers. Ratio analysis takes a lot of experience and requires the fullest possible background information.

Ratios express relationships between numbers. Financial ratios may be expressed as numbers, decimals, or percentages.

The common size statement presents every item as a percentage of the largest item on the statement. Both balance sheets and income statements can be expressed as common size statements.

Liquidity and turnover ratios measure, respectively, a company's ability to pay debts on the basis of current assets and the effectiveness of the company's use of current assets.

Leverage (or solvency, or overall debt and equity) ratios are used as a group to indicate the size of creditors' claims on assets relative to owners' claims on assets.

Profitability ratios employ income statement figures to measure returns relative to various components of the business, such as return on sales, return on capital invested, and so forth.

Glossary

Accelerated depreciation Methods of depreciation that put more depreciation in the earlier years of an asset's use. *See* Declining balance and Sum of the years' digits.

Accounts payable Amounts owing to suppliers of goods or services.

Accounts receivable Amounts due from customers created in the normal course of business.

Allowance and write-off method A system that estimates the potential losses from the year-end receivables. During the following operating year, those accounts deemed uncollectible are written off against this estimate. *See* Direct write-off method.

Appropriation An amount, expressed in money, set aside from the retained earnings of a corporation for a specific purpose. This reduces temporarily the opportunity for dividend distribution. (N.B.: No cash is set aside as a result of an appropriation.)

Asset Property that a company owns, paid for or not.

Balance sheet Statement showing the financial condition of a business as of a particular date.

Bank reconciliation An accounting procedure that determines the reason(s) for the difference between the depositor's balance in the cash account and the bank's balance in the same account, if different. An adjusting entry to the depositor's books should be made to reflect the correct balance.

Bond A corporate long-term obligation. *See also* Debenture.

Bond discount The excess of the par value of a bond over the assets received when it is sold. It is used to adjust the interest shown on the bond to the rate of like-quality bonds on the date of sale.

Bond premium The excess of the assets received over the par value of a bond when it is sold. It is used to adjust the interest rate shown on the bond to the rate of like-quality bonds on the date of sale.

Cash Currency and those instruments that can be easily converted to currency.

Cash discount An amount that a company can take off an amount due to a creditor if making the payment by a certain set date.

Chattel mortgage A mortgage on personalty (equipment, etc.).

Check An instrument signed by the payor requesting a depository to give money to the payee. It can be deposited or negotiated for cash.

Common stock The basic stock of a corporation.

Conditional sale Sale of a single item or group of items to be paid off by regular payments until paid. Title does not pass until all the payments are made. *See* Installment sale.

Contra-asset account An asset-valuation account with a credit balance to be subtracted from the asset to determine the net worth of the asset.

Convertible debt A long-term loan payable that may, under certain circumstances, be converted to equity.

Corporation A business owned by one or more persons who have interest in the business evidenced by stock certificate(s). A corporation is considered a legal entity separate from its owner(s).

Credit terms Inducements to the customer to pay an account promptly, usually in the form of a discount. *See* Cash discount.

Current assets Cash or other assets that can be converted to cash within the coming year.

Debenture A corporate long-term obligation, usually unsecured. *See* Bond.

Declining-balance depreciation A method of cost recovery that applies a constant depreciation rate, based on the asset life and a category factor, to the book value of a long-lived asset. *See* Accelerated depreciation.

Depreciation An accounting convention that spreads the cost of a long-lived asset over its economic or physical life, whichever is shorter. *See* Long- lived asset.

Direct write-off method Taking the loss on an account receivable when it is finally deemed that the debtor will not pay. *See* Allowance and write-off method.

Discount on stock The excess of the par value over the assets paid to a corporation when the stock is initially issued.

Dividends Profits distributed to the shareholders of a corporation.

Double-entry accounting The system of accounting that records equal debit and credit entries for every transaction.

Dual signatures A check-signing requirement in which two approved signatures must appear on every check.

Economic order quantity (EOQ) The most efficient and economical quantity of materials or inventories for a company to purchase at one time, given all the circumstances (price, holding cost, etc.), as computed by mathematical formula.

Equity What a business owes the owner(s).

Extend To multiply a unit price by the number of units—so as to arrive at a total value for units in inventory, for example.

FIFO (first-in, first-out) An inventory valuation system that charges cost of goods sold with the oldest costs in inventory. *See* LIFO.

Financial assets Assets that can be quantified and expressed in terms of dollar value.

Finished goods Items in the inventory of a manufacturing business that are completed and ready for sale to customers.

Fixed assets See Long-lived assets.

Income statement Report of the results of business activities over a fiscal period, showing revenues, related expenses, and profit (or loss) for the period. Also called profit-and-loss statement, operating statement, or operations statement.

Installment sale Sale of a single item or group of items to be paid off by regular payments until paid. Title usually passes on date of sale. *See* Conditional sale.

Inventory Assets purchased by a merchandiser to sell or for a manufacturer to use; also, a manufacturer's completed goods and work in process.

Invoice Document from a seller showing what goods or services were delivered, when they were delivered, and the amount due.

Just-in-time (JIT) A newly developed method of raw materials purchasing; attempts to reduce materials inventory and lead time in manufacturing by having all materials arrive on the date that they are needed.

Kiting Procedure used to show a larger balance in a bank account than the depositor actually possesses.

Land A site on which to put an economic facility.

Liabilities What a business owes to nonowners.

LIFO (last-in, first-out) An inventory valuation method that charges cost of goods sold with the newest (usually the highest) costs in inventory. *See* FIFO.

Liquid Usable without conversion to satisfy all obligations— cash, for example. Also, capable of meeting current liabilities—a company with adequate current assets, for example.

Long-lived asset An asset whose useful economic life exceeds a year. *See* Depreciation.

Loss Excess of related expenses over income during a fiscal period.

Mortgage A lien on property, often used to secure a loan.

Net worth *See* Equity.

Nonfinancial assets Assets that cannot be quantified or expressed in dollar terms.

Partnership An unincorporated business owned by two or more persons.

Per-hour depreciation A depreciation method in which an asset cost per hour of asset use is developed. This asset cost per hour of production is then multiplied by hours of service in the period to get the current depreciation expense.

Personalty All nonrealty tangible property. *See* Realty.

Per-unit depreciation A depreciation method in which an asset cost per unit of output is developed. This asset cost per unit is then multiplied by units produced in the period to get the current depreciation expense.

Petty cash fund A small amount of cash used by company employees to pay small incidental expenditures so as to avoid writing checks for these small amounts.

Preferred stock Stock that is paid dividends at a fixed predetermined rate. Usually takes precedence over common stock as to payment of dividends and payment of assets on liquidation. For these preferences, preferred stockholders give up voting rights.

Premium on stock The excess of assets paid to a corporation over the par value when stock is initially issued.

Profit The excess of income over related expenses during a fiscal period.

Proprietorship A one-person-owned unincorporated business.

Realty Land and all attachments to the land. *See* Personalty.

Receivables Any claims a company has against others that are expected to be settled in cash; principally, trade receivables (customers' accounts and notes receivable).

Retained earnings   The account that measures the undistributed earnings of a corporation.

Secured debt   A debt agreement in which the borrower pledges a specific asset as security for the amount borrowed. It can be created on purchase, or later on refinancing.

Statement of financial position or condition   *See* Balance sheet.

Straight-line depreciation   A depreciation method that allocates the same amount of the asset's cost less salvage value to operations each year.

Sum-of-the-years' digits depreciation   A depreciation method that applies a reducing fraction to the asset cost less salvage value. *See* Accelerated depreciation.

Superior claim   A claim (against a business's assets) that takes precedence over other claims.

Trade discount   The discount given to a buyer based on the buyer's position in the merchandising chain (manufacturer, wholesaler, retailer).

Treasury stock   Issued stock of a corporation that is now owned by the corporation and not canceled. It may have been repurchased or may have been acquired in some other fashion. Receives no dividends and has no voting rights.

Universal product code (UPC)   A bar code on a package identifying the manufacturer and the product.

Variance account   Account used to record differences between actual manufacturing costs incurred and standard cost of goods produced.

Voucher   Internal document on which are recorded the vendor's name and address, the amount due (gross or net), the due date of payment, and the approving signatures. Usually accompanies invoice when invoice is presented for payment.

Work in process   A manufacturer's unfinished goods.

Index

Accelerated cost recovery systems (ACRS), 94–95
Accelerated depreciation, 88, 94, 171
Accounting, double-entry, 5–6,173
Accounts payable, 171
  ratios for, 159–160
Accounts payable turnover (APT), 159–160
Accounts receivable, 171
  aging schedule of, 52–53, 54–56, 58
  collections on, 26–27
  ratios for, 158
  See also Receivables
Accounts receivable turnover (ART), 158
Accruals, 106
Acid test ratio, 157
ACRS. *See* Accelerated cost recovery systems
Aging schedule, 52–53, 54–56, 58
Allowance and write-off method, 51–53, 54–56, 171

Appreciation, 98
Appropriations, 144–145, 171
APT. *See* Accounts payable turnover
ART. *See* Accounts receivable turnover
Asset costs, 84
Assets, 4, 17, 172
  liquidity and turnover ratios, 156–160, 169
  nonfinancial, 6, 175
  See also Cash; Inventories; Long-lived assets
Average pricing, 66–67, 80

Balance sheet, 4–6,172
  account form, 6, 7
  comparison of, 14–16
  importance of, 12–18
  report form, 6, 8
Bank reconciliation, 30, 33–35, 172
Bar codes, 26, 61, 176
Benefits. *See* Employee benefits
Billing policies, 47–48, 50–53, 58

177

Bonding (security), 24–25
Bonds, 120–121, 126, 129, 172
Buildings, 84, 97–99, 101. *See also*
   Realty

Capital, 149
Capital gains, 96
Cash, 21–23, 172
  deposits, 22
  disbursements control, 27–32, 39
  petty cash, 31–32, 39
  protection of, 24–33, 39
  receipts control, 25–27, 39
  sources and uses of, 35–37
  unavailable, 22
  valuation of, 22–23
  See also Assets
Cash discounts, 49, 58, 111–112, 172
Cash equivalents, 22
Cash flow, 23–24, 39
  and bank reconciliation, 30, 33–35
  and credit, 49–50, 58
Certificates of deposit (CDs), 22
Chattel mortgages, 119–120, 129, 172
Checks, 28–29, 172
Collateral, 50
Collection period for accounts
  receivable (CPAR), 158
Collection policies, 47–48, 50–53, 58
  allowance and write-off methods,
    51–53, 54–56
  direct write-off method, 51, 173
Common equity ratio, 161
Common size statement, 154–155
Common stock, 141–142, 144, 150,
  172
Conditional sale, 44, 172
Contra-asset account, 51–53, 172
Contract of sale. *See* Chattel
  mortgages
Convertible debt, 116, 121–122, 126,
  128, 129, 172
Corporate veil, 141
Corporations, 140–145, 147–149,
  150, 173
Cost, prorated, 83

Cost value, 63–64, 79
CPAR. *See* Collection period for
  accounts receivable
Credit
  allowing discounts, 49, 58
  billing and collection policies,
    47–48, 50–53, 58
  and cash flow, 49–50, 58
  charging interest, 48, 58,
    161–162, 169
  granting, 44–45, 58
  lines of, 117–188, 126, 128, 129
  problems with issuing, 45–50, 58
  types of, 42–44, 57
  using outside, 53–54, 57
  See also Receivables
Credit cards, 53
Credit terms, 173
Currency receipts, 25–26
Current assets, 5, 173
Current liabilities, 5
Current payables, 105–106, 113
  and cash discounts, 111–112
  control of, 106–110, 113
  rent as, 124
  and trade discounts, 110,
    112–113, 114
Current ratio, 123, 156–157

Debentures, 120, 129, 173
Debt ratio, 160–161
Debts. *See* Long-term debts;
  Short-term debts
Declining-balance depreciation, 90,
  100, 101, 173
De facto corporation, 140
De jure corporation, 140
Depreciation, 82, 173
  of buildings, 84–85
  methods of, 86–95, 99–101
Direct write-off methods, 51, 173
Disbursements control, 27–32
Discounts
  credit, 49, 58
  on loans, 121
  on stocks, 142–144, 173

See also Cash discounts; Trade
    discounts
Dividends, 141–142, 173
Double-entry accounting, 5–6, 173
Dual signatures, 28–29, 173

Earnings report. *See* Income
    statement
Economic order quantity (EOQ),
    70–72, 80, 173
Employee
    benefits, 11, 124–125, 129
    earnings, 106
End-of-year inventory, 62, 64–68,
    76–79
EOQ. *See* Economic order quantity
Equipment, 96–97
Equipment accounts, 85–86, 101
Equity, 5, 6, 17, 149, 173
    and convertible debt, 122
    See also Owners' equity
Equity ratio, 161
Expense account, deferred interest,
    119
Extend, 173

FIFO. *See* First-in, first-out inventory
Financial assets, 174
Financial statements, 12
Finished goods, 61, 174
FIrst-in, first-out inventory (FIFO),
    10, 65–66, 76–79, 174
Fixed assets. *See* Long-lived assets
Formal in-house credit, 43, 57

Goods for sale inventory, 61–62,
    63–64
Gross profit ratio, 162–163
Guarantees, 124

Historical cost, 64, 82, 83, 84
Holding cost, 68–72

Income statement, 6–7, 9–10, 17–18,
    174
    footnotes to, 10–11, 18, 122, 129

Income tax
    and corporations, 140–141, 144
    and depreciation, 88, 94–95
    and disposal of long-lived assets,
        96
    and inventory valuation, 76–78
    and long-lived assets, 81, 84, 101
    and partnerships, 137
    and proprietorships, 137
    and realty, 84
Inflation, 81
Informal in-house credit, 43, 57
Installment contract. *See* Chattel
    mortgages
Installment sales, 43–44, 174
Insurance, 124
Interest
    on bonds, 120–121
    charging, 48, 58
    and times interest earned,
        161–162, 169
Inventories, 59, 79, 174
    average pricing, 66–67, 80
    control of, 68–76
    first-in, first-out, 10, 65–66, 76–79
    last-in, first-out, 10, 65–66, 76–79
    and ratios, 157, 158–159
    security of, 72–76, 80
    types of, 61–63, 79
    valuation of, 63–68, 76–79
    See also Assets
Inventory turnover ratio, 158–159
Invested capital, 143, 149
Invoices, 47, 111–112, 114, 174
Issued stock, 142
Item cost, 68–72

Just-in-time inventory (JIT), 72, 80,
    174

Kiting, 30, 174

Land, 83, 97–99, 101, 174
Last-in, first-out inventory (LIFO),
    10, 65–66, 76–79, 174
Leases, 11, 95–96, 101, 123–124, 129

Leverage ratios, 160–162, 169
Liabilities, 5, 17
  contingent, 11
  current payables, 105–114
  and leases, 95
  and partnerships, 137–138
  See also Long-term debts
Liens. *See* Mortgages
LIFO. *See* Last-in, first-out inventory
Lines of credit, 117–118, 126, 128,
  129
Liquid, 174
Liquidity ratios, 156–160, 169
Loans, 117, 126, 128, 129
Long-lived assets, 5, 10, 81–82, 175
  disposal of, 96–99, 102
  leasing versus buying, 95–96, 101
  types and values of, 82–86, 101
Long-term debts, 5, 11, 106,
  115–116, 123–125, 129
  and leverage ratios, 160–162, 169
  maturity of, 116
  repayment schedules, 116
  special considerations with,
  122–123
  types of, 117–122
Loss, 175

Market value, 63–64, 79
Materials and supplies inventory,
  62–63, 64–67
Money market funds, 22
Mortgages, 118–120, 126, 128, 129,
  175
Mortgages payable, 119
Multiple accounts, 29–30

Net assets, 149
Net profit ratio, 162–163
Net worth, 5, 134, 149, 164, 175. *See
  also* Equity
Noncurrent assets. *See* Long-lived
  assets
Noncurrent liabilities. *See*
  Long-term debts
No-par stock, 143, 144

Operating income ratio, 162–163
Operations statement. *See* Income
  statement
Ordering cost, 68–72
Owners' equity, 133–134, 149
  corporations, 140–145, 147–149,
  150, 173
  partnerships, 137–140, 146–147,
  149–150, 175
  proprietorships, 135–137,
  145–146, 149, 175
  sources of, 134–135, 149
  See also Equity

Partnerships, 137–140, 146–147,
  149–150, 175
Par value, 143
Payment period for accounts
  payable (PPAP), 159, 160
Per-hour depreciation, 90–93, 94,
  101, 175
Perpetual inventory system, 61
Personalty, 85, 175
  and mortgages, 119–120
  See also Realty
Per-unit depreciation, 90–92, 94,
  101, 175
Petty cash, 31–32, 39, 175
PPAP. *See* Payment period for
  accounts payable
Preferred stock, 141–142, 144, 150,
  175
Premium on loans, 121
Premium on stock, 143, 175
Profit, 175
Profitability ratios, 162–164, 169,
  170
Profit-and-loss statement. *See*
  Income statement
Profit sharing, 11
Property
  tax free exchange of, 98
  See also Buildings; Equity; Land;
  Realty
Proprietorships, 135–137, 145–146,
  149, 175

Purchasing cost, 68–72
Purchasing inventories, 68–72, 80

Ratios, 123, 153–155
  groups of, 155–164
  leverage, 160–162, 169
  liquidity and turnover, 156–160,
    169
  profitability, 162–164, 169, 170
Raw material inventory, 159
Real estate. *See* Realty
Realty, 85, 175
  and mortgages, 118–119
Receipts control, 25–27, 39
Receivables, 41–42, 57, 175
  aging schedule of accounts,
    52–53, 54–56, 58
  collection policies, 51–53
  recognizing losses from, 50–53, 58
  used as collateral, 50
  used as cash, 50
  See also Credit
Rent, as current payable, 124
Repayment schedules, 116
Retail pricing method, 63
Retained earnings, 144–145, 150,
    176
Retirement plans, 11
Return on common equity (ROCE),
    164
Return on equity (ROE), 164
Return on total assets (RTA), 163
ROCE. *See* Return on common
    equity
ROE. *See* Return on equity
RTA. *See* Return on total assets

Salvage value, 87
Secured debt, 116, 118–120, 129,
    176
Security systems
  for cash assets, 24–33, 39
  for current payables, 106–110, 113
  for inventories, 72–76, 80
Separation of functions, 25, 26–27,
    28, 30, 39, 47, 106–110, 113

Sole proprietorships. *See*
    Proprietorshiips
Stocks
  premium or discount on, 142–144
  types of, 141–142, 150
  value of, 11
Storage cost, 68–72
Straight-line depreciation, 87–88,
    99, 101, 176
Sum-of-the-years' digits deprecia-
    tion, 88–89, 100, 101, 176
Superior claim, 176

Tax Reform Act (1986), 88, 94
TIE. *See* Times interest earned
Times interest earned (TIE),
    161–162, 169
Trade accounts, 106
Trade discounts, 110, 112–113, 114,
    176
Trade-ins, 97
Trade receivables, 41
Treasury bills, 22
Treasury stock, 142, 150, 176
Turnover ratios, 156–160, 169

Unviersal Product Code, 26, 61, 176
Unsecured debt, 116, 117–118, 129
UPC. *See* Universal Product Code

Variance account, 67, 176
Voucher system, 28, 29, 176

Warranties, 124
Working capital, 24, 39, 123
  and the current ratio, 156–157
Work in process inventory, 63,
    67–68, 176
Write-off methods, 51–53, 54–56,
    171, 173